CUMBRIA LIBRARY SERVICES

COUNTY COUNCIL

This book is due to be returned on or before the last date above. It may be renewed by personal application, post or telephone, if not in demand.

C.L.18

Get DEAD

By Jamie Oliver
Photography by Cristian Barnett

First published in Great Britain in 2006 by Friday Books

An imprint of The Friday Project Limited

83 Victoria Street, London, SW1H OHW

www.thefridayproject.co.uk

www.fridaybooks.co.uk

© Jamie Oliver 2006

ISBN 10 - 1-905548-26-5

ISBN 13 - 978-1-905548-26-2

British Library Cataloguing in Publication Data.

A catalogue record for this book is available from the British Library.

Photography by Cristian Barnett • Design by Jenny Eade

Printed by Graphicom, Italy

The Publisher's policy is to use paper manufactured from sustainable sources.

Get dead? Whether you're making a killing on the stock market, looking forward to murdering a pint or wearing clothes to die for, the fact is, life is crammed with references to death.

Every other news story is to do with death or dying. Each day we are told what foods will kill us, the dangers of riding a bike or the perils of ironing a shirt. If the number of dead is large enough or the story especially bizarre, even otherwise largely irrelevant foreign deaths will grace the pages of British newspapers over the more mundane issues of life and living.

And all this for a topic that is taboo. So much so that no one mentions it at school and no preparation is offered for the emotional, practical or financial impact that death has. And then, shock horror, someone dies!

So this book takes that taboo and gives it a slap. As a guide to death, this book is for the living. It's not a sad book, though. Like all interviewees said, at the end of the day, you've got to laugh...

"Always go to other people's funerals, otherwise they won't come to yours." Yogi Berra

"Millions long for immortality who do not know what to do with themselves on a rainy Sunday afternoon." Susan Ertz (d.1985)

"The idea is to die young as late as possible." Ashley Montagu (d.1999)

"For what is it to die, but to stand in the sun and melt into the wind?" Kahlil Gibran (d.1931)

"The last enemy that shall be destroyed is death." 1 Corinthians 15:26.

"Let us endeavour to live that when we come to die even the undertaker will be sorry." Mark Twain (d.1910)

"Once the game is over, the king and the pawn go back in the same box." Anon

"The poor wish to be rich, the rich wish to be happy, the single wish to be married, and the married wish to be dead." Anon

p9

DEAD SERIOUS

When, how and why you die
Age and ageing, lifespans and longevity. Accidents, crime and punishment. Suicidal tendencies, celebrity deaths, Royalty and famous last words. Death and animals, euthanasia and hospices.
Plus: The Met Police on murder, the BBC on graffiti, motorcycle funerals, an A&E nurse on killing patients and what next for David Beckham?

p49

DEAD CALM

You're dead. Now what?
What happens in the days immediately following your death. Organ donation, pathology, embalming, mortuaries, flowers, obituaries and cryogenics.
Plus: A Home Office pathologist on holy wars and soufflé, a Hindu on reincarnation, a female embalmer, writing obituaries for the living, and why, when and how people kill each other.

p169

DEAD INFO

p89

DEAD & BURIED

The funeral

Funerals in the UK, weird and wonderful funeral directors, cultural differences, cremation, burials at sea and more bizarre methods. Also, what music to choose, disposing of ashes, becoming a diamond, cemeteries and a princess.

Plus: Going green, weedy Anglicans, freelance gravediggers, gypsies, Buddhists, Humanists, rip-offs and graveside punch-ups.

p127

DEAD AHEAD

What now for the living?

Wakes, wills, last wishes and parties. Grieving and gravestones, epitaphs and memorials. Also, where next? Heaven, Hell, reincarnation, immorality, ghosts, cloning and martyrs.

Plus: Human nature and death, getting buried in a guitar, coping with death, swearing at vicars and burying your neighbours. Finally, why do they use such old men as pall-bearers? A salutary tale.

"It's not that I'm afraid to die. I just don't want to be there when it happens." Woody Allen

When, how and why you die

DEAD
SERIOUS

Detective Sergeant Callum Sutherland is a crime scene manager in the Metropolitan Police

Forget the body, it's dead; it's not going anywhere. When you get to the scene of a murder, the first thing to do is to look at the overall picture. Stay neutral. I'm good at my job.

You get used to grim scenes. To be honest, there's so much to think about.

Babies don't bother me. Young kids do, though. The Paddington rail crash, as well. When you're in a mortuary and there are lots of bodies, that is upsetting.

Body parts were found on a golf course in South Norwood, London. The girl was known locally, if you know what I mean. Everyone thought her ex-husband did it until a cabbie came forward and said he'd seen an older guy walking towards the golf course that night, carrying a bin bag. Turns out it was the upstairs neighbour. We found a gun in his flat, an air rifle. He'd cleaned it but it had traces of blood up the barrel. He told us he shot her by mistake and was so frightened he cut up the body. He said it took him two hours. With that bread knife? No chance. We reckon it took him five days.

No one will suspect you if you're walking down the road carrying a bag with a head in it.

The easiest way to get rid of a body is to cut it up.

People don't tend to murder strangers. Most murders are domestic or pub-related. All it takes is too much drink, one punch, down they go, hit their head on the pavement and it's all over. People are murdered for stupid things. Ten pence, a mobile phone.

Sometimes you go to a house, a murder scene, where the wife is dead and you know the husband did it. You just know. What you do is look around the room and see if he then starts looking around the room. You watch his eyes. People give themselves away.

If a police officer is drinking a lot, the force will try and get rid of them. It won't help. Uniformed officers get counselling, but they only do it for the two hours overtime.

I suppose it has affected me. If I hear people moaning about something, I do think to myself that they haven't got anything to complain about compared with others.

I do platform diving. And off the boards. My best move is probably an inward one-and-a-half somersault. It's the closest thing to golf in that if you get it fractionally wrong, you're in trouble.

It's hard to throw someone out of a window. It's hard to hang someone else, too. One case we did was this guy visiting a prostitute. He'd been put into a dog collar and hooked up to the wall while she whipped him. He was on amyl nitrite and loads of Viagra. Anyway, he had a heart attack but she couldn't unhook him from the wall and he hung himself. You shouldn't laugh, but we turn up two hours later and the Viagra's still working!

Deaths requiring counselling

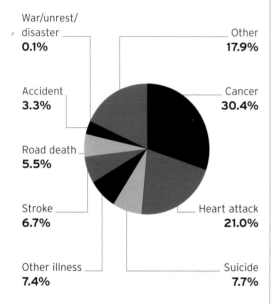

War/unrest/
disaster
0.1%

Other
17.9%

Accident
3.3%

Cancer
30.4%

Road death
5.5%

Stroke
6.7%

Heart attack
21.0%

Other illness
7.4%

Suicide
7.7%

Source: Cruse Bereavement Care

The most common cause of accidental or violent death for males is suicide.

Next most likely is a land transport accident. For women, the most common cause of accidental or violent death is by falling over.

Executions

Tyburn
On 23 June 1649, 23 men and one woman were executed at Tyburn, the largest number of criminals put to death in a single execution in Britain.

One for the road
The gallows at Tyburn stood near present-day Marble Arch, at the north-east corner of Hyde Park, London. Condemned prisoners were transported in open carts along Holborn, St Giles and what is now Oxford Street. Prisoners would be offered wine at various stages along the journey.

Monday feeling
Most Mondays, crowds of 10,000 people attended the executions at Tyburn. A high-profile case could attract up to 50,000. When Arthur Thistlewood and the Cato Street conspirators were executed at Newgate Prison in 1820, an estimated 100,000 watched.

Newgate Prison
It closed in 1902. A total of 1,154 executions took place there: 1,151 hangings and three women were burnt for coining. In all, 49 women and 1,105 men were executed in 119 years.

Bad execution day
Charlotte Corday d'Armont was executed on 17 July 1793 for the murder of Jean-Paul Marat. At the execution the assistant executioner,

Francois le Gros, lifted up the severed head and slapped the cheek, which gave the appearance of blushing. Le Gros was sentenced to three months in prison for his breach of scaffold etiquette.

Dick Turpin

Highwayman Dick Turpin was born in 1706 in Essex. On the run after stealing a horse in London, Turpin fled to Yorkshire. He was arrested for shooting his landlord's rooster

Poison: More than half of all deaths from injury and poisoning in females are at aged 75 and over.

and threatening to shoot the landlord. He was hanged on 7 April 1739 and is buried in the churchyard of St George's Church, York.

Some death-related place names

Killingworth, Tyne & Wear

Deadwaters, Lanarkshire, Scotland

Deadman's Hill, Bedfordshire
On 22 August 1961, a couple were attacked in a lay-by on the A6 at Deadman's Hill, near Luton. Michael Gregsten was shot and killed; his lover Valerie Storie was raped and shot. Storie survived. James Hanratty was convicted of the murder in 1962 and hanged at Bedford Prison on 4 April 1962. Hanratty claimed to have been in Rhyl, North Wales, on the day of the murder. His family waged a long campaign to clear his name. However, in May 2002 the Court of Appeal ruled that the DNA evidence had established his guilt "beyond doubt".

Killington, Cumbria

Coffinswell, Devon
Named after the 12th century Lord of the Manor, Hugo Coffin.

Gravesend, Kent
Final resting place of Native American princess, Pocahontas.

Eva Lunderskov is a junior surgeon

People should show more interest in first aid. Anyone can do it. I sat with a group of friends and not one of them had any first aid knowledge. So if they had a heart attack, they would be alright because I was there, but if I had one, I'd be stuffed!

While a student, I went to London to go on a course in a cardiovascular unit. I was in theatre one day, assisting, when I noticed that one of the medical staff had accidentally cut a hole in the patient's heart. Blood was pouring out of him but no one noticed. I was only a student so I said nothing. Anyway, the nurse soon spotted it and the surgeon came rushing into the room. It was an amazing sight to see. He set up a bypass through the patient's groin, circulating the blood, and that kept him alive while he sewed up the hole. It was like you see on TV. That made up my mind. I wanted to do that.

People rarely walk into A&E and die.

Surgery suits my personality. I think I'm impatient, an instant-results type of person. Of course when you are in surgery you have to be patient, but you get to see results.

My father is a famous actor in Denmark. Everyone there my age would know him from the children's TV show he did. And he was in the famous Danish film, *Festen*.

Two things make you die. Either you stop breathing or your heart stops beating.

I worked in a transplant department in Denmark. You are on call 24 hours a day because, when someone is brain dead, you have less than 24 hours to harvest the organs, as they say. One time, the donor and the recipient were in the same hospital, so I went and took the heart, packed it in ice and took it into another theatre where the surgeons were ready to put it into another man. It was the strongest feeling I ever had. The cycle of life, there and then. It was hard to contemplate, but it was really cool.

I love cooking. Cakes and desserts are my thing, especially raspberry meringue.

A lot of organs go to waste in this country. One person's organs could allow six others to live. I've got a donor card, but no one really talks about it in this country. In Denmark, we are very upfront about it.

If you say no to being a donor, should you be able to receive organs? I don't know.

The heart beats, even if the brain is dead. And the body is still warm. So when removing organs for a donation, in a way, you are killing them. But you go home thinking that you have saved a life with the organs. You have to.

I've told people that their relatives have died. You hope they don't kill the messenger.

In medicine, death is generally seen as a personal failure on the part of the medical staff.

I think I see death in a rational way. Sometimes, things are beyond repair. It's as simple as that.

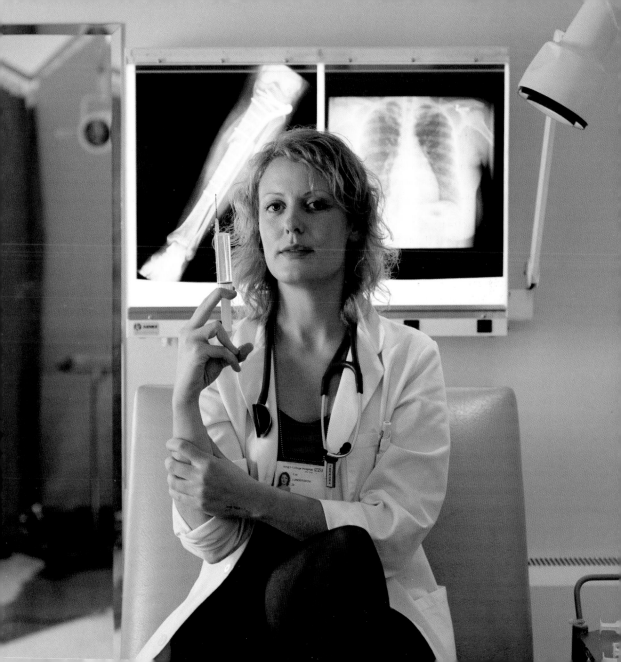

Treason

William Joyce (d.1946), better known as Lord Haw-Haw, was hanged for treason on 3 January 1946, the last person to have been hanged for this offence in Britain. It was a controversial case. Joyce was born in New York and had no duty of allegiance to the Crown so therefore could not be guilty of treason. After a House of Lords ruling, he was hanged at Wandsworth Prison in London.

The death penalty was abolished in 1965

(although treason, piracy with violence and arson in Royal Dockyards remained capital crimes). On 31 July 1998, high treason and piracy with violence ceased to be so-called capital crimes.

Crimes for which burning at the stake was the penalty

- Heresy (opinion or a doctrine at variance with established religious belief).
- Witchcraft (committed by either sex).
- Women convicted of high treason* (including "coining", the clipping of coins for pieces of silver and gold which were melted down to produce counterfeit coins) or petty treason (the murder by a woman of her husband or her mistress).
- * *Men who were convicted of high treason were hanged, drawn and quartered; however, this was not deemed acceptable for women as it would have involved nudity.*

Fans of burning at the stake

- King Henry VIII.
- Queen Mary I (otherwise known as "Bloody Mary"). There were 274 burnings for heresy during her five-year reign (1553-58), including the Archbishop of Canterbury Thomas Cranmer. The normal place of execution in London was West Smithfield (now called just Smithfield).
- The Spanish (especially during the Spanish Inquisition). Shedding a victim's blood was not allowed under the prevailing Roman Catholic doctrine.
- The Scots.

True or false? Nails and hair continue growing after death.

False: The skin recedes, giving the impression of growth.

270,000

Number of heart attacks in the UK each year, according to the British Heart Foundation. Each day, your heart beats about 100,000 times and pumps about 5,000 gallons of blood. You are 80 per cent more at risk of heart disease if overweight.

Smoke?

It is estimated that one in three people will develop cancer at some stage in their lives and that one in four will die from the disease. In 2000, there were 42,800 cancer deaths in the UK attributable to smoking – approximately a third of all cancer deaths. The UK Government has set a target (for England) to reduce the cancer death rate in people aged under 75 by 20 per cent by 2010.

Murder: UK

March 1999–March 2000	760
March 2000–March 2001	792
March 2001–March 2002	891
March 2002–March 2003	1,091*

(This includes 215 attributed to Dr Harold Shipman)

Murder: US

In 2002, 16,110 people were murdered in the US

Rigor mortis *n.*
temporary stiffness of joints and muscular rigidity occurring after death, which lasts for about four days

In the UK, one person every 15 minutes is diagnosed with lung cancer. About 90 per cent of all lung cancers are caused by smoking, either directly or through indirect exposure.

5,268

Number of life-sentence prisoners in England and Wales in 2002, according to the Prison Reform Trust. For the rest of Europe combined, the figure is 5,046. France had only 556 "lifers". Today the lifer population of England and Wales stands at about 5,500. Seven out of ten life-sentence prisoners are serving mandatory life sentences for murder.

RIP George Orwell (d.1950) **is buried at All Saints, Sutton Courtenay, Oxon. Born Eric Blair in Bengal, India, his father worked for the opium department of the civil service.**

Abu Sayeed is a Muslim imam

I go to Great Ormond Street Hospital twice a week. For three hours a time, sometimes more if people want to talk. I visit sick children and their families and provide spiritual guidance.

Death is important, because the afterlife is everlasting. Muslim people are happy to talk about death. We plan for it.

We have a saying: "A true Muslim shouldn't go bed until his will is under his pillow."

Muslims are never cremated. It's disrespectful. The respect we show for the dead body is the same you would show for a living person. So you would never burn a body, or drown it.

In this time of ours, everyone thinks of money. To Muslims, human dignity comes first.

Death is very complex. It has positives and negatives.

I advise and admonish the living, telling them not to worry about losing someone but to be happy that God's will has been implemented. Those who obeyed God in life will enjoy life in paradise. But others, who did not, will face hardship and suffering.

You have no escape from death. Everyone must die.

To believe in an afterlife is a cardinal feature of being a Muslim. There are three cardinal features: to believe in God; to believe in Mohammed; and to believe in a life after death.

Heaven and Hell are a part of our belief. Heaven is an area of bliss. Hell is harsh. If someone is not obedient they will go to Hell. If they are obedient, they go to paradise. If someone has faith, but is not a practising Muslim, they will go to Hell. But after suffering, proportional to the person's sins and misdeeds, they can go to Heaven.

Never walk over the grave. It's respect for the soul of the dead person. Dogs aren't allowed in Muslim cemeteries either.

The sooner the burial, the better.

If a post-mortem is required by law, then it is allowed. And if a Muslim person wants to donate organs it is lawful. But it must be for a purpose.

When you face a sad person, as a human you are sad too.

It is recommended that men visit the graves of deceased people. Not for the dead, but to remind the living that death is a consequence of life.

My advice for a dying person? Make a real turn back to God. I tell people to be ready with a clean heart. If they have done anything wrong they should seek forgiveness from God and from the person they have wronged.

My job is to help people. Big or small help. That's the meaning of life.

Feeling lucky?

You are 20 times more likely to suffer a fatal accident at home than you are to win the National Lottery. It could be you.

Drowning

Overall the drowning rate per 100,000 of population is steady at 0.76. That's about 420 people; 75% of those are male. There are most drownings in August; least in March.

Drowning by location

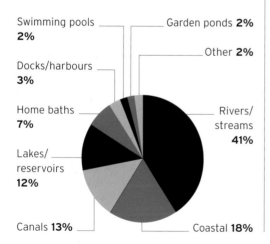

Swimming pools **2%**

Garden ponds **2%**

Other **2%**

Docks/harbours **3%**

Home baths **7%**

Rivers/ streams **41%**

Lakes/ reservoirs **12%**

Canals **13%**

Coastal **18%**

2,498

Number of people who died from accidental poisoning 1901–05.

8,786

Number of people who died from accidental poisoning 1961–65.

Speed kills!

About 1,100 people are killed and 12,600 are seriously injured in speed-related road accidents each year on Britain's roads, according to The Royal Society for the Prevention of Accidents. Roughly two-thirds of all car crashes in which people are killed or injured happen on roads with a speed limit of 30mph or less. At 35mph a driver is twice as likely to kill someone as they are at 30mph. Hit by a car at 40mph, nine out of ten pedestrians will be killed. Hit by a car at 30mph, about half of pedestrians will live. Hit by a car at 20mph, only one out of ten pedestrians will be killed.

Suicide

There are more than 800,000 suicides per year worldwide, according to the Centre for Suicide

Research. In the UK there are approximately 5,000 suicides per year, considerably more deaths from suicide than from road traffic accidents. The number of people presenting to hospitals following deliberate self-harm episodes exceeds the number of suicides in most countries by at least 20 to one.

Not dead

A study of 150,000 exhumed American war dead from the Second World War in Europe revealed that 6,000 (four per cent) showed signs of having been buried alive, according to *The Lazarus Syndrome* by Rodney Davies.

Are they dead or not?
Simple checks

- Listen to heart with stethoscope for five minutes.
- Feel pulse at side of neck.
- Shine a light into eyes to see if pupils stay dilated.
- Touch eyeballs.

Black death: "To our great grief the plague carried off so vast a multitude of people of both sexes that nobody could be found who would bear the corpses to the grave. Men and women carried their own children on their shoulders to the church and threw them into a common pit."

William of Dene, Rochester-based monk, writing in 1349. The Black Death killed between a third and one half of the British population in 1348–49.

RIP Diana, Princess of Wales (d.1997)
Buried at the Althrop Estate, Northants. She is famous for, among other things, shaking the hand of an AIDS patient at the Middlesex Hospital in 1987 and campaigning against landmines.

"Slips and trips are often seen as a joke; however, in reality, nothing could be further from the truth."

Thirty-three per cent of all reported major injuries are slip or trip related.
They cause two fatalities per year. Slips and trips cost employers £512m per year,
the NHS £133m per year and "incalculable human cost", according to the Government.

Kevin Bocquet is the BBC's
north of England correspondent

You can't quote me on that.

Some murders are like a good novel and people like that. If it's got a time element, such as the body is found 20 years on, that makes for a good story. You can also give the story a romantic name, such as the Lady in the Lake.

A boy was murdered on a bus. It was the bus driver, which was unusual, but we had trouble forcing it on. It turns out the boy was allowed to travel on the buses on his own and used to hang around the streets. He was a bit of a street urchin. There is a class element to what stories make the news.

Soham was a story about the State getting it wrong. I mean, we tell our children to go to teachers if they have a problem and then this happens. I think everyone was disturbed by that.

Some murders are entertainment. Some are straight grim.

The most dramatic day of my life was the last day of the Bulger trial, listening to the judge summing up and sitting there watching the scene unfold. The Bulgers are a tough family from Liverpool – from Kirby, actually. They were angry, sad, everything you would expect. More interesting was the reaction of the parents of the two boys. Thompson's mother was in denial. Venables's father Neil, who had come across as fairly tough up to that point, simply collapsed when the judge announced the guilty verdict; his body shuddered with the sobs. He turned to his wife and put his hand on her shoulder seeking comfort, but she ignored him. She sat bolt upright, completely still and expressionless, staring ahead, unseeing. Susan Venables went to stand below the dock, held her son's hand and was whispering to him. But what does a mother say to a child killer, who is also her 11-year-old son?

The Radio 4 audience is indiscernible from people who read PD James and watch *Inspector Morse.* Fifty years ago, these people used to be into diamond heists, now it's murder. It's all about the psychology of the murderer. People love a murder mystery story.

Shipman was interesting. The sheer scale was unbelievable. But there wasn't anything like the revulsion to him as there was to others, like Fred West. Dame Janet Smith I think summed it up best in her first report. She said he had a compulsion to kill and a compulsion to stop. He got caught due to a ridiculous faked will. He wanted to be caught.

The One O'clock News crowd are into graffiti. They want to hear about graffiti, litter-dropping and low-level crime. And the odd murder.

I love this job.

Virginia Woolf (d.1941) **filled her pockets with stones and drowned herself in the River Ouse, Sussex. The suicide note read:**

"I feel certain that I am going mad again: I feel we can't go through another of those terrible times. And I shan't recover this time. I begin to hear voices, and can't concentrate. So I am doing what seems the best thing to do. You have given me the greatest possible happiness... I can't fight it any longer, I know that I am spoiling your life, that without me you could work." The Letters of Virginia Woolf, vol. VI, p. 481.

William Campbell (d.1878): Known as the heaviest man in Britain at the time, Campbell died aged 22 weighing 53 stones (chest: 96in). He died on the third floor of a public house and the spectacle of removing the body was a compelling sight. Between 30,000 and 40,000 sightseers watched the funeral procession. He was buried at Jesmond Cemetery, Newcastle.

Fame
Peg Entwistle (d.1932), US actress, was the first person to jump to their death from the letter 'H' of the Hollywood sign in Los Angeles.

Shoplifting was a capital crime in 1699

Dead people who adorn banknotes
£5. Prison and social reformer Elizabeth Fry (d.1845).
£10. Charles Darwin, naturalist, author of The Voyage of the Beagle (d.1882).
£20. Edward Elgar, composer (d.1934).
£50. Sir John Houblon, first Governor of the Bank of England (d.1712).

Alice Molland was the last woman to be hanged for witchcraft in England, in 1684.

Britain at war

Battle of Britain: Churchill declared it had started on 18 June 1940. British aircrews numbered 2,440 (there were 510 pilots from overseas). During battles with Germany, 507 were killed. In the House of Commons, 20 August 1940, Churchill said: "Never in the field of human conflict was so much owed by so many to so few."

Battle of Balaklava: A breakdown in communication during the Battle of Balaklava (1854) led to British commanders sending the Light Brigade to attack strong Russian positions. Roughly a third of the 673-strong brigade were casualties. The episode is a fine example of military stupidity.

Zeppelin: German airships attacked Britain in 1915. On 19 January, two Zeppelins attacked the eastern coastal towns of Great Yarmouth and King's Lynn, killing four civilians. A further seven people were killed in the first Zeppelin attack on London on 31 May. In 51 raids, they killed 556 people and injured 1,357.

Falkland Islands: The 1982 conflict cost 236 British lives and 750 Argentinean. The islands were named after Viscount Falkland (d.1689), a one-time treasurer of the British navy.

"And now, in keeping with Channel 40's policy of always bringing you the latest in blood and guts in living colour, you're about to see another first – an attempted suicide."

The final words of Christine Chubbock (d.1974), a US news reporter, who shot herself live on air.

The Reverend Paul Sinclair, the "faster pastor", runs Motorcycle Funerals

I'd rather regret having tried and failed at something than not having tried at all.

I was born in Glasgow and wanted to work in the shipyards, so did an apprenticeship as a sheet metal worker aged 16. I worked at Govan and Yarrow.

I can't say I had a revelation. God uses natural things to bring out the supernatural. I did feel as though I had a calling, then one of the men I worked with said something that changed my life. He said: "If Tarzan can train a monkey, then God can do something with you."

Why do I live in Leicester? I'm no more than three hours from any mainland mortality.

I worked at a church in Willesden, north London. I remember a girl called Joan. The hospital told her she had a malignant tumour behind her ear so we prayed for her. After further tests, the tumour simply disappeared. The doctors were amazed - everyone was, to be honest. You have to decide whether you believe that or not, but I definitely believe it was a miracle. Of course, I've prayed for many people who have seen no change in their condition.

Ask for forgiveness first, permission later.

Disorganised religion is worse than organised religion, but many churches are competing with God, not serving Him.

I've faced fierce opposition. I was 16 when I became a Christian. Imagine working at a shipyard and admitting that? It was torture, horrendous. My family was embarrassed and you become a social nightmare. Everyone thinks you are weird and waits for you to make a mistake.

Steve McQueen got me into motorbikes. Jumping over that fence. Everyone says having a motorbike is dangerous, but I'll tell you something. My friend had a motorbike and he had four friends who did not. They have all died of various diseases and he's still alive.

What I really want is a factory so I can manufacture hearse sidecars. I've got the technical skills to do it but need investment. Then I could lease them out.

Hells Angels. What better congregation to have than one that knows where it is going? It's even written on their backs! But they are straight with you and they've got great integrity.

Every motorcyclist knows it could be his or her last ride. I think that's why there is an openness to spirituality in the biker world.

I've got a friend who is a Humanist. The funny thing is, he's struggling with his atheism!

One day you will stand before God. All of us will be found wanting. I really believe that. There are no unbelievers except among the living.

Christianity and death

British tradition has it that few public tears are shed at funerals and hysterics are kept to a minimum. Although few people attend church, most opt for Christian-based services, either in a church or a crematorium. Horse-drawn hearses are witnessing a revival and expensive and elaborate floral displays are commonly seen. It is traditional to wear dark clothes to funerals and black ties with suits.

Old-timers

Chapter five of Genesis describes six Biblical figures who lived over 900 years, including Adam (930 years) and Methuselah (969 years). Noah (of Ark fame) lived 950 years, according to the Bible. Genesis (Chapter 11) lists four people who lived more than 400 years.

Life expectancy

- In 2004, life expectancy at birth for females born in the UK was 81 years, compared with 77 years for males.
- Between 1970 and 2004, life expectancy at age 65 increased by four and a half years for men and three and a half years for women.
- At present there are more people aged 70 and 80 than ever before.
- Life expectancy for women in the UK passed the 80-year mark for the first time in 2000. Men lag five years behind. The English tend, year on year, to live longer than the Welsh, and both live longer than the Scots.

Dead already

Funeral directors and crematorium managers complain that the death rate is falling. One reason put forward is the Second World War. So many of those who should be dying now are already dead.

Better lot for babies

Death rate for babies under a year

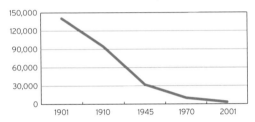

Total deaths in 1901 were 551,585
By 2001, total deaths had fallen to 530,373

RIP Thomas Parr (1483-1635) **Parr allegedly lived for 152 years and nine months through the reigns of ten monarchs and was buried in Westminster Abbey by order of King Charles I. His diet was reported to be "green cheese, onions, coarse bread, buttermilk or mild ale (cider on special occasions) and no smoking".**

The Great Fire of London, which started on a Sunday morning, 2 September 1666, in Pudding Lane in the City of London, destroyed 373 acres inside the city walls and 63 acres outside. Eighty-seven churches (including St. Paul's Cathedral) and 13,200 houses were razed to the ground. Where the fire stopped at the corner of Giltspur Lane and Cock Lane in Smithfield, a statute was erected, the Fat Boy, representing the vice of gluttony – supposedly the cause of the disaster. It was originally built into the wall of the Fortune of War public house, which in the 18th century became a notorious haunt of the resurrection men or bodysnatchers. Only six people are thought to have been killed by the fire, which put an end to the Great Plague.

RIP **John Fuller (d.1834) A wealthy eccentric, he is said to have had a "burning desire" to be remembered long after death and went about ensuring this by erecting various structures, including a wooden lighthouse at Beachy Head, Eastbourne. Known as "Honest John" or "Mad Jack", he is said to have been buried sitting upright, holding a bottle of wine and wearing a top hat.**

RIP **Archbishop Parker (d.1575) is buried at Lambeth Palace Chapel, London. Regarded as a busybody in his day and responsible for attempting to set up the first national register of births, deaths and marriages, the Archbishop is said to be the man behind the phrase "Nosey Parker".**

...Death news...

Up to 150 graves in St Woolos Cemetery, Newport, may not contain the body of the person named on the headstone, the local council revealed in 2002.

A 70-year-old man collapsed and died at the wheel of his car in a Gloucester cemetery in October 2003. The pensioner's car rolled into two other vehicles, one of which knocked into a woman standing nearby. She was not seriously injured.

A couple who already have permission to use part of their land as a cemetery are refused permission to turn their bungalow into a private crematorium. Conwy Council refused the application after hearing a 220-name petition against the development. One neighbour, who did not want to be named, said: "I think the idea is bizarre and completely ridiculous. People around here have been dead against the crematorium and it has caused a lot of bad feeling."

Melcombe Regis (Weymouth) Cited as the port through which came the Black Death, otherwise known as the Plague, in 1348. The plague devastated much of Europe throughout the Middle Ages. The Great Plague of London (1664-66) killed 70,000 people in south-east England.

Deborah Annetts is chief executive of Dignity in Dying

I think you understand life backwards. It takes strange paths. Doing this job was never inevitable, though as I look back it all fits into place.

I was brought up with socialist values that you should always help people. When I finished university I started working in the NHS as a management trainee. I worked in every department and, one Monday morning, I witnessed eight post-mortems back to back. I'll never forget that.

I worked with cancer patients and remember seeing people having to grapple with the end of their lives. One lady had bone cancer. She was a very religious lady, a Christian, but in enormous pain. She was on so much morphine that it was giving her delusions that she was about to be taken by the Devil. She was traumatised by the pain relief. That can't be right.

Almost immediately after joining Dignity in Dying I got a call from Brian Pretty, Diane Pretty's husband. She was amazing, brave, fearless and took her case all the way through the UK and European courts. All she wanted was respect and the right to help to die. People say Diane died a natural death, but what happened to her was appalling. I was with her when she died. She was on six morphine pumps to stop her screaming from the pain she was in.

Respect is such an important thing in all of this.

Eighty-two per cent of people say the law should be changed. People are scared of doctors.

A woman called us. Her mother, blind, deaf, incontinent and in pain, was in hospital. She indicated to her daughter that she did not want invasive surgery to keep her alive. But the doctor said, "I'm going to put a peg-feed into your mother's stomach". It's an appalling way to feed someone. If it was done to a prisoner it would be all over the front page of The Guardian. Done behind closed doors, in hospital, by a doctor, and it's called medicine.

Doctors like to be the ones who decide to withdraw treatment from someone, not the other way round. Many doctors are religious, but if they believe in an afterlife, why don't they allow people to die with dignity? They should be keen to let people die. Doctors are more scared of death than anyone.

People don't go around wanting to die. People strive to live. The concern that people will all suddenly attempt a mass suicide is nonsense.

Catholics talk about life being God-given. But what about those who don't believe? What about the fact that God gave people freedom of will?

When you're terminally ill, it's hard to kill yourself. Your veins shrink; it's harder to swallow. But suicide and wanting to die a dignified death are two completely different things.

It's hard to say what the future holds.

Euthanasia

In England and Wales a person who assists in the suicide or attempted suicide of another is liable to imprisonment for up to 14 years. In Belgium, Switzerland, Germany, France, Sweden, Finland and, where assistance is provided by a medical practitioner, the Netherlands, assisted suicide is not an offence.

Law breakers

Almost half of the public is ready to break the law to help loved ones die, according to an NOP survey. Eighty-two per cent of public support a change in the law on medically assisted dying.

18,000

The number of terminally ill people in Britain who are helped to die by their doctors each year, according to Dr Hazel Biggs, director of medical law at the University of Kent and author. Fifteen per cent of UK doctors admitted to helping a patient to die at their own request.

A survey of 1,000 British doctors found that 45 per cent of them believe that their colleagues are helping terminally ill patients die.

The average 90-year-old's brain weighs 10% less than a 20 to 30-year-old's. An average person in their 90s has only half the lung function of someone in their 30s.

www.deathclock.com

Work out how long you have left. For example, the Prime Minister, Tony Blair, is set to die on Monday 15 February 2027, according to the site.

Living Wills: for and against

A living Will is a document that sets out a patient's wishes regarding health care and how they want to be treated if they become seriously ill and unable to make or communicate their own choices.

Case for: Respect for patient's human rights; doctors more likely to give appropriate treatment; help medical professionals to take difficult decisions; saves family and friends from hard decisions.

Case against: Writing them may be very depressing; difficult to imagine what they would really want in the situations where a living Will would take effect; patients may change their minds.

Last words

"I wish I'd drunk more champagne." John Maynard Keynes (d.1946).

"I have a long journey to take and must bid the company farewell." Sir Walter Raleigh (d.1618).

"Pardonnez-moi, monsieur." Marie Antoinette, Queen of France (d.1793). As she approached the guillotine, she accidentally stepped on the foot of her executioner.

"Get my swan costume ready." Anna Pavlova, ballerina, (d.1931).

Women live a long time

According to Office for National Statistics records, in 1901 there was a category for people living to be 85 or older (a total of 12,607 people lived to be more than 85 years old). Today, there's a category for 85 to 89-year-olds, for 90 to 94-year-olds and one for 95 and over. A total of 21,877 people lived to be 95 or over in 2001; 17,981 of those were women.

There are more than 19.8 million people aged 50 and over in the UK. The number is projected to increase by a further 37 per cent by 2031, when there will be close to 27 million people aged 50 and over. Three local authority districts have more than 30 per cent of people above State pension age: Christchurch, Rother and East Devon.

In the US more than $12bn is spent each year on cosmetics to disguise or prevent ageing. Sun damage is probably responsible for 80 per cent of skin ageing. If it wasn't for the sun, people would not develop wrinkles until they reached their 80s.

Where dead famous people are buried

Emily Davison (d.1913) Buried, Morpeth, Northumberland. A militant women's rights campaigner in 1909, she threw rocks at the then Chancellor of the Exchequer, David Lloyd George, resulting in a month's hard labour at Strangeways prison. She died in 1913 after throwing herself in front of King George V's horse, Anmer, at the Derby in the name of the suffragette movement.

Sir Francis Drake (d.1596) Buried at sea off Portobelo, Panama. Sailor, navigator, privateer or pirate, Drake terrorised Spanish shipping in the 1500s. They called him "El Draque" or "The Dragon".

Sir Richard Tempest (d.1488) buried St Alkeda's Giggleswick, North Yorkshire. Said to be buried with the head of his favourite horse.

Oliver Goldmeyer is chairman of a Jewish burial society

Jewish people must be buried as soon as possible, within the hour, if you can, because as long as the body is outside the grave the soul suffers. The quicker the body rots, the better for it. My mother-in-law died at 1am. She was in the ground by 5am. But then that was a frantic night.

A body must be watched after the person is dead. I think this can be traced back to the old days when things were less hygienic, when there were rats and mice, but it's a tradition that has continued. There are societies of watchers, professional watchers who, for money, will come round and do the watching.

I'm chairman of a burial society. I'm married with children now, so I'm semi-retired. It's considered an honour to be a member of a burial society. It's called a "true kindness", since the person you are doing the kindness to can never repay you.

Jewish law states that there is a period of seven days' forced mourning called Shivah. Psychologists tell me that it's a very wise thing that the Rabbis did. Many non-Jews try to carry on as if nothing has happened, to be strong, to get back to work quickly, but that will always backfire in the end. The seven-day mourning takes place in the house where the person lived. During this time, the mourners cannot leave the house and they must sit on the floor or on stools. Also, all mirrors are covered. A person looks in a mirror to see if they look nice. During mourning, though, it's not about that person, it's about the one who has died and all thoughts must be about them.

Music cannot be listened to for 30 days following a death. We don't have a radio or TV and only listen to Jewish music anyway, so it's not that bad. A TV licence man came round to our house recently and my five-year-old son answered the door to him. The man asked about the TV and my son asked him: "What is a TV?"! The man couldn't believe it.

I have a feeling that, in the next world, David Beckham won't be so important.

We call the afterlife the world of truth. A Jewish cemetery is called a House of Life.

People called Cohen – from the lineage of Moses' brother – cannot go anywhere near a funeral or even a cemetery. Friends of mine called Cohen will get out of the car and go another way if we are passing near a cemetery. Really.

To us, Hell is a system of embarrassments. No one cares about misdeeds here on earth; people can always justify themselves. Even Saddam Hussein would say he was righteous. Over there, misdeeds are brought before other souls and there is no hiding from it.

I used to go to Edgware Hospital every evening to speak to the sick people. Sometimes to give them a kick up the arse. One guy, he had problems with his heart and thought he was dying. I told him to get a grip and, soon after, he came out of hospital. Ten years later I still see him and he still thanks me.

Christine Kalus is a clinical psychologist based at The Rowans Hospice, Portsmouth

I've been interested in death since I was a child. I think because it's about learning how to live. There's something about knowing about finitude. I don't know if you ever understand death.
I've worked in Winchester, Southampton and Portsmouth, predominantly in mental health. I started getting frustrated about how older people were being treated. I was hearing more and more stories about unsatisfactory deaths. It was heartbreaking. I'd been working for years in bereavement making sod-all difference. I wanted to be part of something that really made a difference. So I started working at The Rowans Hospice in Portsmouth.
Once you know about death, you can never not know about it again.
People are reluctant to be referred to a hospice. They see it as doomy and gloomy. But when they come, people say "isn't it a bright place?". Once people have been in contact with a hospice, they are very generous.
The dead rely on the living for immortality.
I met a successful businessman at the hospice. He came here with his son, a teenager, who died. The man had gone through life not really thinking about others and I'll never forget what he told me. He said: "I would never have chosen to have my son die, but the gift of his death has been to make me a better person." But it's not all happy ever after. Some people become stuck. I become tearful, yes, but that's alright. I don't take away people's personal stories.
Families are often caught up with the symptoms and they forget about their relationship.
It's very rewarding to help people move through grief. It can be very consuming though.
You get three to five days' compassionate leave in this country. I find that extraordinary. It's appalling. We need to be kinder; organisations need to be kinder.
Freudian ideas of attachment are important. The attachments made in early infancy are vital. They are strong and they dictate how we relate to people throughout our lives. If we have secure attachments, we tend to be more secure in ourselves. If people have unclear relationships, loving, then not loving, they tend to have ambivalent views of themselves.
"Coming to terms with grief?" I don't know what that means. "Letting go and moving on?" Rubbish.
Why would I want to be anywhere else?
If a man's wife dies, there's an increased risk of heart attacks. For women, there's an increased risk of gynaecological cancers. No one knows why. Research says that the immune system is suppressed for up to two years following a death of someone close. People become susceptible to colds. It's the stress. It has a physical impact.

"Experience is a great advantage. The problem is that when you get the experience, you're too damned old to do anything about it."

Quote, Jimmy Conners.

Famous deaths

Presumed dead in airplane crash: Amy Johnson (d.1941); Glenn Miller (d.1944).
Alcoholism: Jack Kerouac (d.1969); Billie Holiday (d.1959); Truman Capote (d.1984).
Choking: Jimi Hendrix (d.1970); Tennessee Williams (d.1983).
Death by skiing: Sonny Bono (d.1998).
Falling from a horse: Ghengis Khan (d.1227).
Nosebleed: Attila the Hun (d.453) allegedly had a nosebleed on his wedding night and bled to death.
Dead heat: Jockey Frank Hayes (d.1923) suffered a heart attack during a horse race at Belmont Park, New York. The horse, Sweet Kiss, went on to finish first, making Hayes the only deceased jockey to win a race.
Hanged: Screaming Lord Sutch (d.1999) hanged himself following the death of his mother the previous year. He posed the question: "Why is there only one Monopolies Commission?"

RIP Queen Boudicca (d.62/3? AD), **who took on the Romans, is said to have committed suicide by drinking from a poisoned chalice. Legend has it she is buried under a platform at London's King's Cross Station.**

Most missed people in the UK

1	Princess Diana (d.1997)
2	John Lennon (d.1980)
3	Mother Teresa (d.1997)
4	John Peel (d.2004)
5	Churchill (d.1965)
6	Nelson (d.1805)
7	The Queen Mother (d.2002)
8	Your own family
9	Elvis Presley (d.1977)
10	Tommy Cooper (d.1984)

Worst things about dying

- Don't find out what happens in Eastenders/Coronation Street.
- Miss next season's FA Cup third-round giant-killing acts.
- Eternal damnation.
- Your relatives divvy up all your worldly goods (but give most to the charity shop).
- Not telling people what you really think of them.
- No more golf/bingo/gardening/DIY.
- Being reincarnated (as a worm).

Blue plaque deaths

Dress designer Laura Ashley (d.1985) Fell down the stairs at her daughter's cottage in the Cotswolds.

Dr Thomas John Barnardo (d.1905) Died of angina pectoris (lack of oxygen supply to the heart muscle) in Surbiton.
Enid Blyton (d.1968) The author of more than 700 popular children books, died in her sleep at a Hampstead nursing home, aged 71.
Edith Cavell (d.1915) A pioneer of British nursing, died by firing squad in 1915. A statue of her, dressed in a nurse's uniform, looks down to Trafalgar Square, London, from St Martin's Place. She was buried in Norwich Cathedral.
Sigmund Freud (d.1939) The founder of psychoanalysis, died of cancer of the jaw.

Florence Nightingale (d.1910) She arranged for herself and 38 other nurses to be sent to the military hospital in Scutari during the Crimean War. The death rate dropped from 42 per cent to 2.2 per cent. Nightingale was 90 years old when she died. She is buried at St. Margaret's, East Wellow.

TE Lawrence (d.1935), of Lawrence of Arabia fame, died after falling off his motorbike while swerving to avoid a group of children.

Sherlock Holmes creator Sir Arthur Conan Doyle (d.1930) The writer died from heart disease at his home in Crowborough, Sussex. He was originally buried in the garden of his home, but was later moved to the village churchyard at Minstead, in Hampshire.

Sir Robert Peel (d.1850) Home Secretary, founder of the Metropolitan Police Force and responsible for the term "Bobby", died after being thrown from his horse.

Howard Jonas runs the Cambridge Pet Crematorium

One guy came here with his African parrot. It had lived more than 40 years and when he came in he was devastated. He'd known it three times longer than he'd known his wife. There's a huge amount of emotion attached to pets. People grieve for a pet probably more than they do for a person.

Ray Hale and Clive Jackman set up the company in 1979. Ray used to be a rag-and-bone man, going around the East End of London collecting waste materials, such as metals and bones – that is, dead animals.

There are about 11 million cats and dogs in the UK kept as pets. Then there are horses and the more exotic pets. Twenty years ago, people kept larger dogs. Today the demographics have changed and people prefer cats. It's in part down to how people live. With both partners working, there's no one to look after a dog. A cat will look after itself.

Twenty years ago, most people got buried. It was the same with pets. That's changed because of the space available and now it's mostly cremation.

People are either cat, dog or rabbit people. I'm a dog man, although my wife was savaged by a dog when she was a girl and won't go near one. Even if she hears a dog bark she'll lock the doors to the house. My sons and I are trying to change her view, but it's not easy.

Pets never ask where you've been.

The ownership of a dog in a divorce case can be very important. If you think that some dogs live to be 18 years old, that's longer than most marriages.

One old guy travelled from Southampton on his 50cc moped with his dead dog in the basket. He couldn't go on the motorways and it took him 18 hours to get here. We cremated the dog for him and two hours later he set off home.

The largest gathering we ever had for one animal was 40 people.

If it walks, swims or creeps, we can cremate it. From spiders to elephants. We've done about 30 elephants. Lions and tigers, snakes, alligators, giant tortoises, bird-eating spiders, armadillos, anteaters. Burmese mountain dogs can grow to 19 stones, you know.

Guide dogs and police dogs can be difficult. Many people who are mentally handicapped rely on pets and when they die it can be very hard. They don't understand.

People never query an undertaker as to whether the ashes they get back are their loved one's. I get asked that 100 times a week. Everyone asks.

When we do snakes there is very little left. They're all cartilage – apart from the jaw.

We've got the ashes of a vet in the grounds. He'd never really liked people and had always got on better with animals, so he asked to have his ashes scattered here, with the animals.

"Animals have these advantages over man: they never hear the clock strike, they die without any idea of death, they have no theologians to instruct them, their last moments are not disturbed by unwelcome and unpleasant ceremonies, their funerals cost them nothing, and no one starts lawsuits over their wills."

Voltaire, letter to Count Schomberg, 31 August 1769.

Famous dead cats

- Spokes, Eleanor Roosevelt's cat, died when husband FDR ran over her in his wheelchair.
- Elvis, owned by John Lennon. After Lennon's death in 1980, Elvis went to live next door in Mia Farrow's apartment.
- Jock, Winston Churchill's ginger cat, was mentioned in the PM's will.
- Foss. Edward Lear, famous for the limerick *The Owl and the Pussy Cat* had a cat named Foss. When it died, he was buried in Lear's Italian garden.

Rats

Black rats (*Rattus rattus*) have been blamed for spreading the bubonic plague during the Middle Ages.

Fleas (big thighs)

These blood-sucking parasites have the potential to spread dangerous diseases to humans and other animals. A flea can jump up to 200 times its own body length. It can also jump about 130 times its own height. Fleas can live up to a year.

Crows' feat

Since ancient times, crows have been linked with negative forces, especially witchcraft. A crow seen flying around a house or sitting alone symbolises that misfortune is present. If a flock suddenly abandons a nesting area, hard times are said to be ahead. Crows developed a sinister reputation in the Middle Ages by feasting on bodies left on the battleground – and at the gallows. A group of crows is called a murder.

Horses

- Copenhagen, the Duke of Wellington's horse, was buried with full military honours.
- Red Rum is the only horse in the history of the Grand National Steeplechase to win the race three times. He was second twice. Red Rum was buried on 18 October 1995, in a grave next to the winning post at Aintree racetrack, Liverpool.

Living creatures' lifespans (in human years)

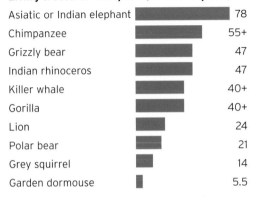

Asiatic or Indian elephant	78
Chimpanzee	55+
Grizzly bear	47
Indian rhinoceros	47
Killer whale	40+
Gorilla	40+
Lion	24
Polar bear	21
Grey squirrel	14
Garden dormouse	5.5

Old birds (ages in human years)

Oystercatcher	36
Black-headed gull	32
Mallard	29
Mute swan	21
Starling	20
Swallow	16
Wren	7

9 lives: Studies show that if a cat falls off the seventh floor of a building it has a 30% less chance of surviving than a cat that falls off the 20th floor. It supposedly takes about eight floors for the cat to realize what is occurring, relax and correct itself.

The oldest goldfish in captivity, Tish, died at the age of 43 after being won at a funfair. It was buried in a yoghurt carton at the bottom of his owner Hilda Hand's garden, in Thirsk, north Yorkshire.

Dog's life
Being buried first or last in a graveyard was frowned upon from the 19th century onwards, often leading to conflict between grieving families (and sometimes resulting in rioting and death). Superstition had it that the first person buried was somehow tied to the Devil. Dogs were often buried before any humans to circumvent the problem. Duties of the most recently buried included all "the onerous tasks of those already buried", including keeping watch over the graveyard until the next funeral.

RIP Isambard Kingdom Brunel (d.1859) **Buried in Kensal Green Cemetery, London. Once, in 1843, while performing a conjuring trick, he accidentally swallowed a coin that lodged in his windpipe. Eventually, Brunel was strapped to a board, turned upside-down and shaken until the coin came out.**

RIP Charles Cruft (d. 1938) **Buried in Highgate Cemetery, London. The dog lovers' first show was in 1891 in The Royal Agricultural Hall, Islington, London. The show is now run at the NEC, Birmingham, attracting crowds of up to 120,000 people.**

"Don't send me flowers when I'm dead. If you like me, send them while I'm alive."

Brian Clough (d.2004)

You're dead, now what?
The next few days...

DEAD
CALM

DECEASED FULL NAME

Dr Ian Hill is a senior Home Office forensic pathologist

I've always been interested in trauma. I started out in the air force, dealing with aeroplane accidents. It's about solving problems, really. I'm interested in the people that survive, too.

There is an inevitable mortality. It's a trite thing to say, but if you say we're here for three score years and ten and that's it, I'd say that was odd. Science doesn't have the answer to the question "why?" But there must be an ulterior motive for man's existence.

I'd be an emotional cripple if I wasn't moved by what I see. While I was working in Kosovo, I saw things that made me wonder about the inhumanity of man.

Holy War is a contradiction in terms. It strikes me as bizarre that people kill in the name of God.

High-profile cases are often the least rewarding professionally. I don't know why some cases get media attention and others do not. You'd have to ask the newspapers that.

Science isn't as good as we think it is. There is a condition, or group of conditions, where people simply drop down dead. It's called Sudden Adult Death syndrome. And no one knows why it happens or how.

Suicide is peculiar in that it requires proof beyond reasonable doubt. But unless there's a note it's impossible to say what was going on inside that person's mind. If someone leaps from a building, what's to say they didn't change their mind halfway down?

If a man drops dead in the street, did he have a heart attack or did he have a malignant tumour? You'll never know until you look.

Baby deaths are the most harrowing because of what they are. But they are also extraordinarily complex. The cause could be something genetic and we're not the best-trained people in these cases. Few pathologists will tackle a post-mortem on a baby alone. The Government is considering training up specialists in paediatric post-mortems.

My family tells me that I'm a bad patient. There are two types of patient. One that requires telling to not put any pressure on a broken leg and another that knows the risks and limitations. I'm the latter. I'm like a motor mechanic. I hear a funny noise under the bonnet and know what it is.

They say a man that has himself for a lawyer has a fool for a lawyer. It's the same with medicine.

The number of autopsies I've done? I don't know. Tens of thousands? I don't count.

I sat next to a Norwegian lady at dinner once. As a country, Norway is big on thanatology, the study of death. All through dinner she talked about it. It was the most inappropriate subject to discuss over the soufflé and it ruined my appetite. Plus, she was a complete bore.

Body find: the clues

Warm and not stiff:
Not dead more than a couple of hours.
Warm and stiff:
Dead between a couple of hours and half a day.
Cold and stiff:
Dead between half a day and two days.
Cold and not stiff:
Dead more than two days.

Autopsy

Also known as a post-mortem examination or necropsy, autopsy is the medical investigation of a corpse. The term comes from the Latin for "seeing with your own eyes". The term "necropsy" is from the Latin for "seeing a dead body". The body is opened and the main organs removed, weighed, inspected and dissected.

What's the point of an autopsy?

To discover the cause of death, to determine the state of health of the person before they died, and whether any medical diagnosis and treatment before death was appropriate.

Autopsies may also be carried out for the purposes of medical research – where permission has been given. An autopsy takes between two and four hours and is at no cost to the family.

Who does them?

Autopsies are performed by specially trained physicians called pathologists.

Who gives permission?

Next of kin or the legally responsible party. A doctor will ask you to sign a consent form to give permission for the autopsy. You may limit the autopsy in any manner you wish. Note: if the cause of death is unclear, the pathologist may perform an autopsy without the family's permission.

Autopsy results

The first findings from an autopsy are usually ready in two to three days. The doctor can review these results with you. A final report may take many weeks because of the detailed studies performed on tissue samples. The doctor will also review the final report with you.

Pathology joke

The psychiatrist knows nothing and does nothing.
The surgeon knows nothing and does everything.
The pathologist knows everything...
....but is always a day too late.

Post-mortems

A glossary of terms

- **Archiving:** the long-term preservation of tissue or organs.
- **Body parts:** groups of organs or a limb or part of a limb.
- **Coroner:** the coroner is required by law to investigate deaths due to unnatural, suspicious or unknown causes.
- **Fixing:** the hardening of organs and tissues by immersion in a chemical, usually formaldehyde. This is so the tissues and organs can be examined in detail under a microscope.
- **Full post-mortem examination:** involves examination of the brain and other parts of the skull and all the contents of the chest and abdomen.
- **Inquest:** these are held by coroners when death is known or suspected to be due to anything other than natural causes.
- **Incision:** a cut in the skin, enabling the body to be opened.
- **Medical Certificate of Death (Death Certificate):** this document enables the registrar to issue a form permitting disposal of the body. It also gives the cause of death; this is important for recording the incidence of diseases in the UK.
- **Mortuary:** a group of rooms, usually in a hospital (those outside hospitals are called public mortuaries), where bodies are kept in refrigerators before collection by undertakers. The mortuary also includes the post-mortem room where the examinations are performed.
- **Pathologist:** a medical doctor trained in the diagnosis and study of disease.
- **Technician:** a person, often a scientist, with special training to assist pathologists in the diagnosis of disease.

There are two types of post-mortem:

1 Post-mortem examinations required by coroners. These are investigations required by law and do not require the agreement of relatives. They are performed to investigate sudden and unexpected deaths; death where the cause is unknown and the doctor cannot issue a death certificate; death where the cause of death is known to be, or suspected to be, due to causes other than natural disease, for example accidents and industrial diseases.

2 Consented post-mortems. These are requested by doctors or by relatives. Full signed agreement must be given by the relatives for this type of post-mortem to be carried out. Relatives can make restrictions for this type of post-mortem. Relatives should be fully informed before giving their agreement.

Keeping organs

Pathologists sometimes wish to keep organs for research purposes. The pathologist, on behalf of the hospital, becomes the custodian of the organ, which is then kept in safe and secure conditions in the hospital. The identity of the organ and the diagnosis remain confidential.

Chandu Tailor is a Hindu funeral director

In India, the job of funeral director is done by "The Untouchables". There is something of a taboo. But, not being born in India, I am a little bit outside of that way of thinking.

If you commit sins in life, it will take 8,400,000 lives before you are reincarnated as a human.

The more illiterate a person is, the more organised they tend to be with their affairs. My uncle was an accountant, for example, but he didn't have a Will.

I love this job. I live at the office more than my own home. In fact, I am going to the Ideal Home Show to buy a modular house that I can assemble in the warehouse so I don't have to go home at all. Don't tell my wife!

The worst aspect of the job is not being able to turn a job around. Sometimes, if someone has had a run-in with an Intercity 125, there is nothing that can be done to make the body look good. The family simply cannot see the body. Saying that, I haven't had a gory one for a while.

We have two big fans blowing air through our embalming room, but even that is not enough sometimes.

People occasionally want to fly the bodies back to India to be burned. You have to use stronger embalming fluid and put them in a zinc-lined coffin. The bodies go on passenger flights, but in the cargo. We don't turn up at check-in time with the coffin!

The Ganges is a ferocious river. It cleans India as it goes along. I'd say 50 per cent of ashes go to India to be scattered in the Ganges. I've been sent out there to scatter ashes for people.

It takes about 40 man-hours to do a funeral. And, at £1,500, I think that's value for money, especially compared with the US or Canada.

The motto is: "Have hearse, will travel... anywhere!" Heh, heh, heh...

A Hindu widow is buried in white, a married woman in red, preferably. If you are burying a single man, you dress them as you would a groom.

It's traditional to carry the coffin and even to touch it is considered good luck. It's seen as a blessing from the person in the coffin. We put whole coconuts in the coffin for the long journey ahead. The Zoroastrians, on the other hand, consider it very bad to touch a coffin.

It takes 13 days for the soul to leave the body.

Women used to throw themselves onto the funeral pyres of their husbands, but that's illegal now.

Traditionally the oldest son organises the funeral of a parent, but Hindus no longer trust their children to do anything for them. So more and more of them are organising their own funerals while they are still alive. The average attendance at Hindu funerals is about 150-200 people.

We're number-plate freaks in the funeral industry.

Swedish biologist Susanne Wiigh-Masak recommends having your body freeze-dried in nitrogen and then shattered to make a soil-enriching powder.

Sikhs believe in an afterlife, when the soul meets with the supreme soul, God (known as Akal Purakh). Cremation is the traditional method of disposal of the body. Death is seen as an act of the Almighty and it is written in the scriptures that emotions should be kept under control so family members may appear detached. The next of kin usually press the button for the coffin to disappear; traditional open-air funeral pyres remain rare events in the UK although, technically, the practice is not illegal as long as certain criteria are met. Ashes are normally scattered in the sea, a river or running water – preferably the River Ganges in India. The mourning period usually lasts between two and five weeks.

Queen Victoria set the fashion for lengthy and strict mourning following the death of Prince Albert from typhoid in 1861. Specific periods of time were considered appropriate. A widow was expected to mourn her husband for at least two years. Deep mourning lasted one year and required not only an all-black wardrobe, but also an extremely circumscribed social life. Jewellery was generally not worn the first year. After one year of deep mourning, a widow progressed to half-mourning and could trade her black crepe dress for a silk one. Half-mourning allowed for jewellery made of pearls, amethysts, black cut glass and jet. After a year of half-mourning, a widow could freely wear any colour. The Queen mourned until her own death.

Body composting

If animal remains, which includes human remains, are mixed with vegetable wastes to the proportion of one in four, in a controlled system, turned and dampened correctly, the result will be a perfect product to be fed to any kind of plant, according to expert Andrew Kerr, quoted in *The Natural Death Handbook*. Note: corpses must be disembowelled in advance and the process takes about 12 weeks. Burying corpses, Kerr suggests, is of no use to trees planted on top since they are buried too deep.

Organ donation

Hinduism: Life after death is a strong belief of Hindus and is an ongoing process of rebirth. The law of karma decides which way the soul will go in the next life.

"It is said that the soul is invisible… knowing this you should not grieve for the body." Bhagavad Gita (Chapter 2:25)

Sikhism: Sikhs believe that life after death is a continuous cycle of rebirth, but the physical body is not needed in this cycle – a person's soul is their real essence.

"The dead sustain their bond with the living through virtuous deed."
Guru Nanak, Guru Granth Sahib, p143.

Islam: In 1996 the UK Shariah Council issued a fatwa (religious opinion) on organ donation. The council resolved that the council supports organ transplantation as a means of alleviating pain or saving life on the basis of the rules of the Shariah.

Muslims and donor cards
The next of kin of a dead person, in the absence of a card or an expressed wish to donate their organs, may give permission to obtain organs from the body to save other people's lives. The fatwa is based on the Islamic principle of al-darurat tubih al-mahzurat (necessities overrule prohibition). Normally, violating the human body, whether living or dead, is forbidden in Islam – but the Shariah believes that this can be overruled when saving another person's life. However, there are also a significant number of Muslim scholars who believe that organ donation is not permissible.

"Whosoever saves the life of one person it would be as if he saved the life of all mankind." Holy Qur'an (Chapter 5:32)

Lucy Howard is training to become an embalmer

People think embalmers have bright red hair, dark rings under their eyes and a hunchback.

Since starting the job I am much more worried about accidents. I'm careful crossing the road, unlike my friends. I'm only 20, so I shouldn't care, but I see the consequences.

To make money in embalming you need to work for yourself. You have to buy all your own chemicals and make-up. It costs between £40 and £100 to embalm someone.

Home Office post-mortems are horrific. They turn people inside out – literally lay people out flat on a slab. When it comes to putting them back together, sometimes you can't. They just fall apart. In one case I did the man had been shot twice and run over twice. He had a Home Office post-mortem and it took seven hours to embalm him. There are a lot of murders in Catford.

When you see horrific cases I can't pretend it doesn't upset me. One week was particularly hard. There was a murder, and a baby death, then a child that had died in a house fire. I got home one night and mum had burnt the dinner. The smell of it made me burst into tears. There's no one for me to talk to about the work I do, apart from my mum.

Death has been mystified by middle-aged men in suits. But death is the most natural thing in the world.

One woman accidentally got her head cut off with a chainsaw – a lady I knew. It was in all the papers. She and her husband had taken a sickie to do some gardening and he was pruning a tree, hit something and dropped the chainsaw on to her. You can't imagine what he must have thought. With most accidents, at least you can call an ambulance and there is some hope.

People look horrified when they are dead. If the eyes are open it can feel intimidating and the gruesome cases can be upsetting. The eyes tell a story about the last thing they saw, and so do their hands. Many will be cut; you can see how they fought for their lives.

Some families can't afford a minister to preside at a funeral but you'll be hard pushed to ever find one who will do a funeral for nothing. It's disgusting. They're only interested in money.

Funeral directors wouldn't give me work experience because I am a girl. They told me that was the reason. Most of them aren't honest with people, they don't care about the families. I want to run my own funeral home, treat people right, be honest with them.

I feel that people sometimes come back to their bodies after they die. I think there's a soul, it goes somewhere, then comes back, just for a moment. I've seen it. The whole atmosphere will change in the mortuary for a split second.

I don't want to be embalmed, it's pointless. You're dead and you're gone I say.

Who's been embalmed?

Vladimir Ilyich Ulynov (Lenin, d.1924) Leader of the Russian revolution, Lenin wanted a simple burial. However, on the orders of Joseph Stalin, his body was preserved for posterity using a secret embalming method. His internal organs were removed. His body was then injected with formalin and immersed in a formalin bath. It was then dried and repeatedly immersed in a bath of glycerine, potassium acetate, water and quinine chloride. Lenin wears a waterproof suit under his uniform that holds in the embalming fluid and his hands and head are bathed in fluid twice a week. His body is still on display in the Lenin Mausoleum, Red Square, Moscow. Entrance: free.

Jeremy Bentham (d.1832) Philosopher and political thinker, Bentham requested that upon death he be embalmed and placed in a glass cabinet at University College London. After problems with his head, though, the real head was replaced by a wax one. The actual head, placed between his feet, was once reported found in a luggage locker at Aberdeen railway station and, more famously, used as a football by college students.

Evita Perón (d.1952) Wife of Argentine dictator Juan Perón. Following a military coup and fearful that Evita's embalmed body (already an object of veneration) could become a symbol of opposition to the new regime, the military first hid it (in a parked truck, an attic, on a naval base) and then buried it secretly in Italy. Years later, the body was returned to the exiled Perón, who proceeded to set up Evita's coffin on his dining room table.

Embalming fluid. What is it?

Formaldehyde, methanol, ethyl alcohol or ethanol, and other solvents.

Only in America

A 1998 research report in Texas, entitled: "A Study of Adolescents' Use of Embalming Fluid with Marijuana and Tobacco", says that users experienced: "Great euphoria or rage, psychedelic apparitions, sleepiness, and forgetfulness."

Going Dutch. In the Netherlands embalming is not allowed except in the case of international transport of the corpse and for members of the royal family, who choose individually for or against it.

> "To medieval man [embalming] meant a process reserved for the preservation of the corpses of the important so that they might sleep uncorrupted in their tombs until the Last Day, when the body and soul would be united to appear before God for His judgement." Julian Litten, *The English Way of Death*.

Die like an Egyptian

Originating in Egypt (6,000 BC), ancient embalming methods included the removal of the brain and viscera, and the filling of bodily cavities with a mixture of balsamic herbs and other substances. The Assyrians used honey, the Persians used wax, and the Jews used spices and aloes. Alexander the Great was embalmed with honey and wax. Some historians estimate that by AD 700 the Egyptians had embalmed approximately 730 million bodies.

"Embalming is about arresting the decomposition," says qualified embalmer Brian Parsons. "Perhaps that's the wrong word. Maybe deterioration is a better one. It also prevents odours or seepages. Embalmers also look after the nose, eyes and mouth of a body, make sure the hair is groomed and sometimes use make-up. One of the greatest compliments you can pay to an embalmer is to say that the person looks like they are asleep. Sometimes, if you are giving them an injection in the face area, you might say: 'This won't hurt.' It's a very cut-throat industry."

[RIP] **William Hunter (d.1783): Scottish surgeon and anatomist was the founding father of modern embalming techniques.**

How to embalm
by Lucy Howard

"Here's how it works. First, clean the body, cut the nails, shave the men (sometimes the women, too!). Then you raise the arteries and pump in embalming fluid at various places around the body. You have to be careful of bulging, especially if they died of circulatory problems. It usually takes about 40 minutes. You watch for the tone of the skin. If someone dies of cancer, for example, the face can look yellow. Embalming gets the colour back. Once the fluid is pumped in, the blood all goes to the major organs. You then puncture each organ and drain the blood from them (heart, lungs, stomach, bladder, throat, etc.). What you don't want is purging – being sick. Then you plug all the holes with cotton wool."

Collin L. Carter runs African-Caribbean Funeral Services

To the best of my knowledge I'm the first black person to be a funeral director in the UK. It's a very positive thing. I consider myself an unappointed ambassador for my race and my community.

In the black community there are more burials than cremation. The reason is cultural, but it's changing and will continue to change. The values and changes occurring in the developed countries are having an impact on the underdeveloped countries. Metropolitan lifestyles will always find a way into developing communities.

Our funerals are considered a community affair and the emphasis is on a celebration of life. It's part of the African tradition and something that 300 years of slavery haven't been able to totally eradicate.

It's part of tradition to see the body and pay the last respects. We express ourselves at funerals in a traditional African way.

I think the strong marketing process has had an influence on funerals. This exhibits itself in the type of hardware people go for now, such as caskets, vehicles and clothing. We have grey cars today. I think people are less inhibited by tradition.

There is a lot of paperwork in this business. Different forms for different circumstances. It all must be checked and you need a good eye for detail. Some of the paperwork must be kept for an indefinite period.

My friends, family and the community were surprised when I started doing funerals. I'm a pioneer and people are generally surprised at any pioneering aspiration or achievement.

The largest funeral I organised in terms of the number of mourners was 2,000. That was for Bishop Bell some years ago.

The most challenging funeral was for Joy Gardner. It was controversial and political, based on the circumstances of her death. All sections of the media covered the funeral; there was a police escort. Everything had to be right.

You have to make sure clients' wishes are executed.

Inflation is up, coffins cost more, fuel costs more, labour costs escalate, everything costs more. So the price of funerals has to reflect that. These costs are not constant.

I have had unusual requests. But that is between the families and myself.

I don't think any community is good at writing Wills. It remains a taboo subject. Most people never feel it is the right time.

If I didn't like this job I wouldn't do it. I get a lot of personal satisfaction from the job and I've made a lot of genuine friends.

To remember me

By US poet, Robert Test

Give my sight to a man that has never seen a sunrise, a baby's face or love in the eyes of a woman.

Give my heart to the person whose own heart has caused nothing but endless days of pain.

Give my blood to the teenager who was pulled from the wreckage of his car so that he may live to see his grandchildren play.

Give my kidneys to a person who depends upon a machine to exist from week to week.

Burn what is left of me and scatter the ashes to the winds to help the flowers grow.

If you must bury something, let it be my faults, my weaknesses and all my prejudice against my fellow man.

Give my sins to the devil. Give my soul to God.

If, by chance, you wish to remember me, do it with a kind deed or word to someone who needs you.

If you do all I have asked, I will live forever.

Firsts...

- 1st cornea transplanted in **1906**
- 1st successful kidney transplant in **1954**
- 1st heart transplant in **1967**

Minority report: poor

People from South-Asian, African and Afro-Caribbean communities living in the UK have a greater chance of needing a kidney transplant than other ethnic groups. This is because they are more likely to develop diabetes or high blood pressure, both of which are major causes of kidney failure. Donation rates are relatively low among black and South-Asian communities, thereby reducing the chance of a successful match being found. Black and Asian people are three times as likely to need a kidney transplant as caucasians.

"Organ donation is an extremely positive action. As long as it is truly the wish of the dying person it will not harm in any way the consciousness that is leaving the body. On the contrary, this final act of generosity accumulates good karma."

Sogyal Rinpoche, *The Tibetan Book of Living & Dying*

Time to go

Corneas can wait up to 12 hours after death to be transplanted. All the rest must be taken immediately after "brain-stem" death.

Rules and risks of living kidney donation

- Must be over 18 years old.
- There is a one in 3,000 chance of death for the operation.
- Long-term risks: small possibility of a slight rise in blood pressure.
- The operation takes approximately two hours.
- Average hospital stay for donor: four to ten days.
- Success rate: 90–95%.

2,867

The highest number of organ transplants ever recorded in the UK was between 1 April 2003 and 31 March 2004. That equates to 1,244 donors. A further 2,365 people had their sight restored through a cornea transplant – the highest number for seven years. One hundred and forty-seven people received lung-only transplants, the highest number ever. During this period, more than 860,000 people added their names to the NHS Organ Donor Register.

What can be transplanted?

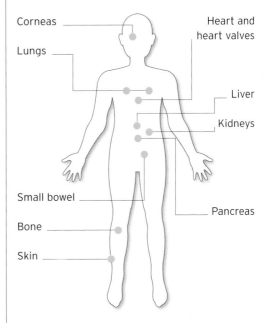

Corneas

Lungs

Heart and heart valves

Liver

Kidneys

Small bowel

Bone

Skin

Pancreas

Note: techniques are constantly improving and it may soon be practical to transplant other parts of the body.

Donating your body to medical science

Contact the anatomy office of your nearest medical school for further details, or HM Inspector of Anatomy on 020 7972 4551. A body can be kept for up to three years.

Michael Burgess is coroner for Surrey and coroner of the Queen's Household

The Queen's Household is like any other area. Like Surrey. The jurisdiction extends to the various royal palaces and residences of the Queen in England and Wales and, as with any other coroner's district, is triggered if there is the body of a dead person lying in the district and the coroner has reason to suspect that the death was due to violence, or was unnatural or sudden of unknown cause. It is not dependent on the status of the dead person.

One in three deaths is referred to a coroner. A trigger is that it's either violent, otherwise unnatural or sudden, or of unknown cause. That's usually the largest reason.

We deal with 4,000 deaths a year in Surrey and there has been a steady increase over the years. I'm not sure one could say one month is busier than another. It's steady.

People often look for answers. But sometimes there is no evidence and no answer. We can't magic answers.

I have families in and have a cup of tea with them sometimes. It helps to explain the verdict. This isn't a totally court-bound service and there's no point in talking in terms that people do not understand. I'm quite sure that any public official has a duty to explain in normal words and give reasons.

Two things are sure. Life can be fragile, but equally humans can be amazingly robust. But also, some people die with very little injury.

I don't like publicity or being photographed.

All of us might think we want this or that at our funeral, or that this sounds nice. I'm sure our families will try to accommodate us. I've never set out on a piece of paper what I want to happen to me. I could write a list today and it will be different tomorrow. Let's just say I'll be looking down or up and thinking what a mess they are making of it. Some people get comfort arranging these things in advance, but I'm not sure I would. Maybe I'll raise it the next time the family plays Trivial Pursuit.

I have six or seven cases a year that involve finds of treasure. In 1984, in Wanborough, someone found about 6,000 gold and silver coins from the Roman era. Another find, in 1986, was hundreds of coins on Reigate Hill. There can be dispute between the landowner and the finder. The Crown, now this means the Government, pays a reward equal to the value of the find.

There may be an interest in death, but I'm not sure people will actually want to buy a book about it.

I can't comment on the Diana case. [Burgess is the coroner in charge of the Diana, Princess of Wales, inquest.]

I don't do extreme sports, although my nephew does. So I suppose vicariously I do. I do the usual things, gardening, writing and reading.

POLICE

Working for a safer London

WE ARE APPEALING

CAN YOU H

MURDER

Royal (and other) deaths

Who?	How?
Harold II	Arrow to eye

This fact is debated. Some reports say Harold escaped the battle and lived out the rest of his life as a recluse in Dover Castle.

William II	Hunting accident

Shot by an arrow. He was possibly murdered.

Henry I	Eating fish

The fish in question was a lamprey, an ocean fish that spawns in fresh water.

Richard I	Arrow wound

Causing septicaemia.

Edward I	Rectal cancer

Probably.

Richard II	Poisoning

Possibly mushroom.

Richard III	Killed at the Battle of Bosworth

He is the only king to have no known grave.

Henry VIII	Renal and hepatic failure

Henry died from obesity. During the committal, it is reported that his coffin "burst forth offensive matter and filled the church with a most obnoxious odour".

Oliver Cromwell	Pyelonephritis

That's an inflammation of the kidney. Considered a traitor following the restoration of the monarchy, Cromwell's body was exhumed and hung on Tyburn Tree and then beheaded. His head was put on a spike at Westminster Hall where it remained for 24 years. After being blown down in a gale, the head was sold to various people down the years before finally being left to Sidney Sussex College, Cambridge, where it rests today.

> The coroner's court is a court of law and, accordingly, the coroner may summon witnesses. People found to be lying are guilty of perjury.

The post of coroner dates from 1194. The duties of the early coroners were varied and included the investigation of almost any aspect of medieval life that had the potential benefit of revenue for the Crown. Suicides were investigated on the grounds that the goods of those found guilty of "self murder" would be forfeited to the Crown, as were wrecks of the sea, fires, both fatal and non-fatal, and any discovery of buried treasure in the community that, as "treasure trove", remains one of the coroner's duties today.

The coroner's job is to determine the cause of death in cases where the death was sudden, unexpected, occurred abroad, was suspicious in any way, or happened while the person was under the control of the so-called central authority, for example in police cells. The most common verdicts from coroners are: death by misadventure; accidental death; unlawful killing; lawful killing; suicide; natural causes; an open verdict.

Most common inquest verdicts:

1 Accident or misadventure
2 Natural causes
3 Suicide

> Where any person is aware of a body lying in the district of a coroner, they have a duty to report it to the coroner. **Failing to do so is a criminal offence.**

What is an inquest?

An inquest is not a trial. It is a limited inquiry into the facts surrounding a death. It is not the job of the coroner to blame anyone for the death, as a trial may do. An inquest is an inquiry to find out who has died, and how, when and where they died, together with information needed by the registrar of deaths. Most inquests are held without a jury (unless the death occurred in prison or in police custody, or resulted from an incident at work).

Anyone who has what is called "a proper interest" may question a witness at the inquest.[1] He or she can get a lawyer to ask questions or they can ask questions themselves. Questions must be "sensible and relevant". This is something the coroner will decide. Speeches are not permitted.

[1] *A parent, spouse, child and anyone acting for the deceased. Anyone who gains from a life insurance policy on the deceased. Any insurer having issued such a policy. Anyone whose actions the coroner believes may have contributed to the death, accidentally or otherwise. The chief officer of police. Any person appointed by a Government department to attend the inquest. Anyone else who the coroner may decide also has a proper interest.*

Famous TV coroner

Dr R Quincy, played by Jack Klugman. Klugman was also "juror number five" in the 1957 film 12 Angry Men in which a Latino boy is accused of killing his father.

Carol Thomson is Bath's most experienced florist

It's a shame more people don't send flowers to people when they are still alive. The best reason to send flowers is no reason at all.

When someone walks into the shop you have to work out very quickly his or her state of mind. It could be flowers for a wedding, new baby or funeral.

Funerals can be very divisive for families when it comes to the flowers. Everyone tries to outdo each other.

People swap the cards on funeral tributes. It's incredible but I've seen it.

A woman came in to buy a single red rose. An hour later another woman came storming into the shop demanding to know a description of the woman who had just placed a single red rose on her husband's grave. I told her we sold a lot of single red roses and the girl who had sold it was out. I wasn't about to give her a description.

We've done funeral tributes in the shape of poodles, rugby balls, taxis, boats, a goldfish, a pair of scissors, a violin, a snooker table, a smiley face, even a chef's hat. We used cabbage leaves as the base for that one.

Florists are prone to arthritis. And, because you're standing up all day, varicose veins.

Orchids are my favourite. I'm not keen on double chrysanthemums.

My dad was a plane fanatic. We used to live in Purley and go to Heathrow to watch the planes coming in. But we'd wait up to three hours to see one! That was 40 years ago but you can't believe it now. Transport has revolutionised the flower industry.

Don't buy me flowers! Wine, yes.

Jack Dee got it right when he said: "It's kind of garages to supply buckets for people to put their dead flowers in."

You don't send carnations to an Italian or chrysanthemums to a Spaniard. Both are associated with funerals.

There are no black flowers. I think the nearest thing I've seen is something called a bat flower.

All cut flowers are dying really. People often don't bother using the sachet that comes with flowers but they should.

If you're going to leave flowers at the scene of an accident, don't leave the cellophane.

A lady came into a friend of mine's shop after her husband had died. She asked the florist if she could do a floral tribute in the shape of his tool. My friend's jaw dropped before the woman quickly added that he used to be a plumber. She wanted it in the shape of one of his plumbing tools.

People think foliage grows on trees.

Don

I would like to
to live after

Let your relatives know
and keep this card with you

Rt Rev Richard Harries is the Bishop of Oxford

There's been a big change in the way the church deals with death. In the 19th century, the church stressed the afterlife, but now most clergy act as bereavement counsellors. Bereavement is part of the job.

We can't describe death. I believe there's life after death. It's the consummation of the divine purpose.

It's a privilege being a priest, being with people at the highs and lows of their lives.

During the committal at one funeral, a woman rushed to the front and started clinging to the coffin to stop it going through the curtain. It was a very poignant moment.

My parents were not great church goers, actually, and I never went to Sunday school. Gradually, the church took hold of me. I felt a very strong sense of calling. My family were pretty shocked, as I hadn't really talked to them about it. They thought I was going to muck-up my life.

The post of Bishop of Oxford goes back to the Reformation and Henry VIII. He cut this diocese out of the Lincoln Diocese. It's amazing to think that now. But unless I become Archbishop of Canterbury, there's nowhere else for a bishop to go.

If I get an invitation to speak at a tiny church in the area, I'll go. There are 820 churches in this diocese and 800 clergy.

I'm never home in the evenings.

Christianity has become a foreign language. The last time England was really a religious country was during the time of the Civil War.

There's not just a decline in church attendance. There's a decline in voting, trade union membership and football match attendences.

Heaven is the presence of God. You create your own Hell.

I don't do many funerals now. I did one recently, though. It was a teenager, stabbed to death. I think because it was quite high-profile they wanted me to do it. About 200 of his mates came but it was very difficult to find the right language. I felt out of my depth.

I used to play tennis, but my hips aren't really up to it.

Almost any graveyard is evocative.

I'll probably be cremated. I want my ashes to be buried in west Wales, where my family were from.

I spent four years in the army, but my only enemy while in Germany during the 1950s was the soot and the cold. I never shot anyone.

Transplants

Christianity: Sacrifice and helping others are consistent themes in Christianity, which teaches the principle of seeking for others what you hope others would do for you. Matthew, Chapter 10:8:

"...freely you have received, freely give".

Judaism: In principle, Judaism supports and encourages organ donation in order to save lives. Jewish law requires consultation with a competent Rabbinic authority before consent is granted.

"One who saves a single life – it is as if he has saved an entire world."

Pirke D'Rav Eliezer, chapter 48.

Christian funerals

There are up to 220 different Christian denominations in the UK (rituals may differ). Christians believe in the resurrection and the continuation of the human soul, in Heaven. Many churches have specially written funeral services, as well as special readings, prayers and hymns. Some funerals may include a special service called Holy Communion, Eucharist or Mass that recalls the last supper that Jesus Christ shared with his disciples before his death.

Lacrimation *v.* the body's process of producing tears, which are a liquid to clean and lubricate the eyes. The word lacrimation may also be used in a medical or literary sense to refer to crying.

But what is crying?

There are three basic types of tears.

- In healthy mammalian eyes, the cornea is continually kept wet and nourished by basal tears.
- Reflex tears come as a result of irritation to the eye by foreign particles or substances such as onion vapours.
- The third type of tears, called crying or weeping, is increased lacrimation because of strong emotional stress or pain.

Tears brought about by emotions have a different chemical make-up than those for lubrication. It has been suggested from their stress hormone content that tears may be a method of expelling excess hormones from the body.

Crying game

Although chimpanzees, elephants, dogs and bears can shed tears, scientists doubt whether this is an emotional response. To weep crocodile tears is to pretend a sorrow that one doesn't in fact feel, to create a hypocritical show of emotion. The idea comes from the ancient belief that crocodiles weep while luring or devouring their prey. Despite the saying, crocodiles don't shed tears.

Songs that make you cry

Danny Boy, (Trad)
He Stopped Loving Her Today, George Jones
Old Shep, Elvis
One Less Bell to Answer, 5th Dimension
The Little Boy That Santa Claus Forgot,
Nat King Cole
Candy Says, The Velvet Underground
Nocturne in G Minor, Friedrich Chopin
The End of the World, Skeeter Davis
At Seventeen, Janice Ian
Carrickfergus, Van Morrison
Women's Prison, Loretta Lynn
Brick, Ben Folds Five
I Still Miss Someone, Johnny Cash
Unwed Fathers, John Prine

RIP Roy Kelton Orbison (d.1988), famous for the song "Crying", was born in the oil town of Wink, Texas. Elvis Presley called Orbison "the greatest singer in the world", while Barry Gibb of the Bee Gees referred to Orbison as the "Voice of God".

Orbison suffered his fair share of personal tragedies. His first wife, Claudette, died in a 1966 motorcycle accident. Two years later, the family home in Tennessee burned to the ground while he was touring in England, and two of his three young sons died in the fire. In 1973, Orbison's older brother Grady Lee Orbison died in a motor vehicle accident in Tennessee on his way to visit Roy for Thanksgiving. Orbison himself died aged 52 of a heart attack while visiting his mother. He was also well known in the much smaller world of radio-controlled model aircraft as a champion modeller and flier.

What to wear?

At Christian funerals it is traditional for both men and women to wear dark clothes. Celebrities tend to wear sunglasses to funerals to make people think they are grieving (most are also using them to look around for other celebrities/photographers).

It is not obligatory to have a religious funeral or attendant vicar, and anything can be said or sung at a funeral or during the committal. It is not necessary to have a funeral at all.

John Sheils is a senior mortician

I don't ever want to go to hospital. If the nurses don't kill you, the superbugs will. I haven't got a helluva lot of faith in the medical profession. But if you'd seen the things I have, neither would you.

Being a mortician is like working with a wax effigy.

We do about 1,200 post-mortems per year. All sorts. Routine, suicides, suspicious deaths, murders. We did 11 post-mortems this morning. I should spend more time doing paperwork, but I still enjoy the post-mortem room immensely.

There are a lot of television companies making programmes about this business at the moment. It's cheap. I mean, the corpse isn't going to ask for any money!

I don't dislike anything about this job. I wonder if I'm sick in the head. They've tried to put me into counselling but I don't need it. Well, I don't think I do!

I feel it's nice to, sort of, get the body in, do what has to be done, do the job and restore the body to how it was. We wash the hair and blow-dry it, sometimes. That is a bit weird, I agree.

My wife's a nurse. She kills them, I cut them!

You've got to have a sense of humour to do this job. We're respectful, of course, but if you don't laugh, you end up drinking too much and there's even been the odd suicide. You have to make light of a tragic situation. We go in there and take the piss out of each other.

In the summer, when it's warm, people go stupid. They kill each other. If there's a period of leisure time and people are off, in my experience, they tend to kill each other a lot more.

I had a body here for three years once. Normally it's the family dragging things out a bit, something to do with a guilty conscience. At the end of the three years, though, she'd been in and out of the freezer so many times, thawing and refreezing, that you could almost pour her down the drain. I mean, are you telling me that these people quarrelling were her loved ones?

You don't get used to the smell. Sometimes the police use a Vicks inhaler under their noses to mask the smell. But if they read the bottle, they'd see it clears the sinuses! It's all up here [taps head].

People die of everything. I've seen fit and healthy people that have dropped down dead for no reason, and drinkers or smokers who live to a good age. I'll go my own way thanks very much.

The only strange thing I've come across is something I've seen twice. The transposition of organs. Everything that should be on the left is actually on the right, and vice versa. Odd thing is that the two cases I saw, there was no record of it in their medical files. It's like they never knew.

I was born a Roman Catholic but no, I don't believe in anything. Life after death is a big con. When you see a body that's been lying around for eight months, it's hard to believe there's an afterlife.

Taphephobia *n.* an abnormal and persistent fear of being buried alive or of cemeteries.

The fear of being buried alive was real in Victorian times. Some requested that their heads or major arteries be severed, or their heart extracted. Contraptions employing bells, buzzers and flags were devised to send distress signals from buried coffins.

Mortuary

The term formerly meant "a customary gift claimed by, and due to, the minister of a parish on the death of a parishioner". The gift was usually the "second-best animal" of the deceased, or the second-best "moveable object".

The Murder Act 1752 enabled judges to order that murderers' bodies could be dissected after death. In the 18th century, anatomy sessions were held publicly. All the bodies were executed prisoners. The Anatomy Act 1832 stopped murderers' bodies being used in this way, and from then on they were buried at the jail.

The Anatomy Act 1832 stated that medical schools could use any unclaimed corpses (not just those of criminals) once 48 hours had elapsed. The Act put most bodysnatchers out of work.

Suicide

Britain has one of the highest suicide rates in Europe. Each year in the UK more than 5,000 people take their own lives. The Samaritans estimate that in the UK there is a suicide every 82 minutes. The charity Depression Alliance estimates that each year there are about 19,000 suicide attempts by UK adolescents.

Each day, two people under the age of 24 commit suicide. One reason is thought to be because males choose more lethal (and thus successful) methods of suicide, such as hanging, shooting or jumping in front of a train. In the UK, suicide has taken over from road accidents as the number one cause of death for young adult males in the age range 18-24.

Résumé
US poet Dorothy Parker (d.1967)

"Razors pain you;
Rivers are damp;
Acids stain you;
And drugs cause cramp.
Guns aren't lawful;
Nooses give;
Gas smells awful;
You might as well live."

Suicide methods depend on country.

Top ten suicide prisons
(Total suicides for 1995-2004)

1	Manchester	(27)
2	Leeds	(25)
3	Winchester	(23)
4	Durham	(23)
5	Norwich	(23)
6	Nottingham	(23)
7	Liverpool	(22)
8	Preston	(21)
9	Lewes	(21)
10	Birmingham	(20)

Source: Howard Reform Trust

Belgium has more jumping deaths on account of the tall buildings.

Guns are most popular in the US.

Poisoning and hanging are popular in India.

Some places or methods become "suicide magnets". The reporting of suicides often leads to copycat suicide attempts, especially at famous landmarks.

804 and rising

Number of people who committed suicide while in the care of the prison service in England and Wales in the last ten years. Of those, 55% were on remand, despite remandees only comprising 19% of the total prison population. Women were 30 times more likely to commit suicide in prison than in the community. Unfortunately, prisoner suicide reduction is rarely a vote winner.

Aristotle considered suicide an act of cowardice and the Romans legislated against it. Christianity is against suicide on the grounds that it violates the sixth commandment: "Thou shalt not kill."

Andrew McKie is obituaries editor at *The Daily Telegraph*

All life is here.

We occasionally run obituaries for people who aren't dead. By mistake. One was for Dorothy Ritter, wife of US country music singer Tex Ritter. She was ill in hospital and was moved into a different room. A nurse, just back from leave, walked into the room and on not seeing Dorothy asked a colleague where she was. The other nurse replied "she's gone", meaning she'd been moved. Anyway, the nurse took it to mean she was dead and called a friend in the UK and it went from there. Her son called up and told us his mother wasn't dead. She is now. So is he, actually.

I was lucky. On my first day a big one came in. I said, "right, I'll do it". And I did, from scratch.

You can't libel the dead.

I like the fact that you never know what's coming next. And you're writing about people you know nothing about. You have to know a lot of people and if you don't know them, know someone who does.

I have a strong preference for funny over clever.

Who gets in is a lot down to gut instinct. Was the person in *Who's Who?* Did he get knighted? If you're given an honour, there's a case for doing an obituary. But then if you've had a number one single and everyone's heard of you that's also good enough. A huge plus is someone who did two or three different things. Say they were an actor, then a singer, then a pig farmer.

With this job, you don't know what you're looking for.

You don't have to be significant. If the person was a sword swallower, that's interesting.

I'll definitely do Saddam Hussein, Osama bin Laden, Chemical Ali and Gerry Adams. I'll get a lot of calls the following day, but the point is, are these people interesting? Did they do something? I will do Ronnie Biggs because he's part of the culture of this country, but we didn't do Myra Hindley. The rights and wrongs have nothing to do with it.

I was on the letters page the day Diana died. They had information on her but it wasn't up to date. Since she died in the middle of the night, the timing was better for us.

We keep up-to-date files on people such as the Prime Minister, the Chancellor, US presidents, but you can't keep up on everyone. We panicked when we heard Clinton was going in for a heart op because our file wasn't up to date.

There are some stock phrases. "Didn't suffer fools gladly" (bastard). "Convivial" (drunk). "Never married" (that says something about a person, whereas "unmarried" is a fact).

The obits page is one of the most important in *The Daily Telegraph*.

The Pope was ready and poised for years.

An Act of Parliament in
1823 put an end to the
practice of burying suicides
at some public highway
with a stake driven through
them. Suicide was only
decriminalised in the
UK in 1961.

Famous suicides

Eva Braun (1945) Mistress of Adolf Hitler.

Brutus (42 BC) Roman politician, assassin
of Julius Caesar.

Tony Hancock (1968) British comedian.

Boudicca (1st century) Queen of the Iceni.

Ted Moult (1986) TV celebrity, double-glazing
advert superstar.

Some reasons for getting national newspaper obituary:

- Internationally or nationally known figure.
- Local bigwig.
- Highly respected in chosen field.
- Recipient of awards (OBE, knighthood etc.).
- Celebrity (major or minor).
- Achieved something of note while alive.
- Military personnel.
- Acquaintance with newspaper editor.

Tips on writing an obituary
Be sure the person is dead.
Be honest. Not too honest.
Check your facts.
Remember your audience.

Post-funeral drinking venues

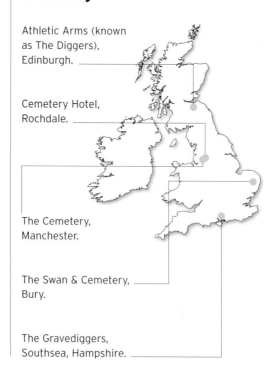

Athletic Arms (known
as The Diggers),
Edinburgh.

Cemetery Hotel,
Rochdale.

The Cemetery,
Manchester.

The Swan & Cemetery,
Bury.

The Gravediggers,
Southsea, Hampshire.

"23 February 1669. I had the upper part of her body in my hands, and I did kiss her mouth, reflecting upon it that I did kiss a Queene, and this was my birthday, thirty-six years old, that I did kiss a Queene." Samuel Pepys, the famous diarist, on an audience he had with the embalmed body of Katherine, Queen of England.

Last drink

The prison surgeon could offer a condemned person their last drink. This was usually a glass of whisky or brandy to calm their nerves. The surgeon also then checked to see that the person was dead after hanging.

Cocktails at the wake?

- **Grateful Dead** (1x rum, 1x tequila, 1x vodka, 1x gin, 1x Chambord, a black raspberry liqueur. Method: Mix all shots into a tumbler with ice, strain into four shot glasses.)
- **Kid Killer** (1x peppermint liquor, 1x tequila, 1x lime schnapps. Method: Pour the peppermint liquor into the bottom of a shot glass, followed by the tequila and then the schnapps. Make sure that the layers do not mix. Drink through a straw as a shot.)
- **Dead Dog** (1x Bourbon, 1x beer, 3 dashes Tabasco sauce. Method: Add in the order given and drink.)
- **Dead DJ** (1x Bourbon, 1x crème de cassis. Method: shake with ice, pour into shot glass.)
- **Dead Mexican's Ass** (1x tequila, 1x milk. Method: drink as shot.)
- **Dead Frog** (1x Kahlua, 1x Baileys, 1x crème de menthe (clear). Method: put the ingredients into a mixing glass on ice, shake and pour.)
- **Dead Lawyer** (1x crème de cacao (dark), 1x Martini bianco (dry), 1x Maraschino liqueur. Method: Fill a shaker half full with ice cubes. Pour all ingredients into shaker and shake well. Strain drink into a cocktail glass and serve.)
- **Drop Dead** (1x Aftershock (blue), 1x Jagermeister, 1x Absinthe. Method: layer in a shot glass gently, drink and possibly drop dead.)
- **Dead Chicken** (1x vodka, 1x egg. Method: wake up, pour vodka into glass, followed by whole egg. Add a dash of tabasco and pepper, then a splash of Worcester sauce.)

The burial of the dead is taken very seriously in Chinese societies. Improper funeral arrangements can wreak ill fortune and disaster upon the deceased's family.

"There's nothing quite so good as burial at sea. It is simple, tidy, and not very incriminating"

Alfred Hitchcock (d.1980)

DEAD & BURIED

Roslyn Cassidy runs Green Endings, an environmentally aware funeral directors in London

It's obvious to me that things to do with loss, be that of a job, partner, or a death, are dealt with badly. We're all sitting on a stack of losses and sometimes the death of someone close opens the floodgates. I think Protestantism offers the least options for healing.

I wasn't prepared for dealing with dead bodies. You might think that sounds strange but I was unprepared for the total stillness. I do talk to the bodies. I think about who they were, their size, what they've done in their lives. But I'm a practical person. I can fix my own boat engine.

My peers treated me scathingly, partly because I'm a woman. They all said it wouldn't work.

It's important for the family to participate in a funeral. People who come and view the body beforehand benefit enormously. They never regret it. Sometimes people are furious. They feel like they've been left behind, there may be unresolved issues or unpaid debt. Some of them really rage at the body and it can go on for hours. I tell them to keep going. One young man shouted and shouted at the body of his father, came out, had a cigarette, then went back in and shouted some more.

People don't know what they believe. But most believe in a superior being.

Babies aren't any harder to deal with, but there's a lot of sentimentality about children, a lot of hope in them. Somehow the order's not right and it jolts people. When people see a little one dead, they think: "It should have been me, the sinner." To me, every human is important, whatever the age. One family came in with their 97-year-old mother and they were devastated.

Girls get together and talk. Boys play football. From an early age boys are taught not to cry or face up to their emotions and it's predominantly men that kill themselves. If there is a suicide in the paper, you'll see there is a flurry of suicides. People copy so you should be very careful.

When it comes to funerals, many people often do the minimum. I helped one lady organise a funeral for her mother. Afterwards though, she told me that she had always hated her mother and wasn't paying for it! I get people to sign a contract now.

A green funeral can be anything. They are popular because people are aware of the environment and want a personalised event. There's a lot of talk about lack of burial space, but actually, there's loads of space.

Middle-class people will say they want a simple service but really they mean cheap.

The cost of flowers for funerals is a scandal.

Up to 70% of people never visit family graves.

"Magnificent Seven" cemeteries in London
- Kensal Green (opened 1832). Privately owned.
- West Norwood (1837). Lovely.
- Highgate Cemetery (1839). Costs £2 to enter.
- Nunhead (1840). Beautiful woodland, good for walking, pushing prams and exercising dogs.
- Brompton (1840). Occasional suspicious characters frequent this cemetery.
- Abney Park (1840). Sometimes frequented by alcoholics.
- Tower Hamlets (1841).

Funeral procession etiquette
Old days: slow down, stop, doff cap, bow head. These days: honk horn, flash lights, attempt to overtake.

[RIP] Johnny Morris (d.1999) **presenter of** *Animal Magic*, **was buried at home with his old zookeeper's cap.**

Winston Churchill's pallbearers
The Right Honourable Mr Harold Macmillan
Field Marshall Viscount Slim KG.
Marshal of the RAF. The Viscount Portal of Hungerford, KG.
Earl of Avon, KG.
Field Marshall, Sir Gerald Templer KG.
The Right Honourable Sir Robert Menzies, KT.
The Earl Attlee KG.
Field Marshall The Earl Alexander of Tunis, KG.
The Lord Normanbrook, GCB.
The Lord Bridges, GCB., GCVO., MC.
Admiral of the Fleet, The Earl Mountbatten of Burma, KG.
The Lord Ismay, KG.

[RIP] **Novelist** Dame Barbara Cartland **was buried on 24 May 2000 in a cardboard coffin in the grounds of Camfield Place, her home near Hatfield in Hertfordshire, near a 400-year-old oak tree that was planted by Elizabeth I. Mourners took oak leaves from the tree as a memento.**

You³ An urn or casket for cremated remains should be of sufficient internal dimensions to provide a minimum of 200 cubic inches (3,280cm cubed).

Top 10 funeral songs

1 *Fields of Gold*, Eva Cassidy.
2 *Always Look on the Bright Side of Life*, Monty Python.
3 *Nothing Compares to You*, Sinéad O'Connor.
4 *I Did It My Way*, Frank Sinatra.
5 *My Forever Friend*, Charlie Landsborough.
6 *Another One Bites the Dust*, Queen.
7 *Ring of Fire,* Johnny Cash.
8 *Puff the Magic Dragon*, by Peter, Paul and Mary.
9 *Danny Boy*, traditional Irish song.
10 *You'll Never Walk Alone,* music by Richard Rodgers, lyrics by Oscar Hammerstein.

DIY funerals

Get buried in your garden

Planning permission is not strictly necessary if you wish to be buried in your own back garden. One or two burials in a garden is acceptable, but check deeds for any restrictions. Consult the local planning office and environmental health department (they will want to ensure that the local water table will not be affected). *Note: a burial at home could bring down the value of your home, for obvious reasons. Consider the implications of moving house.*

How to organise a DIY funeral

- If a person dies at home you can normally keep the body there for a couple of days simply by turning off the heating in the room and by opening the windows.
- If the person dies in hospital, arrange a time to pick up the body with a sister present. Sign a release form. Note: ask the mortuary staff how many assistants you will need to bring.
- Rent or borrow a van or estate car. Arrive with a coffin you have bought or made.
- Before the funeral you will need to register the death with the local registrar (see phone book).
- If using a crematorium, ensure you fill out the correct forms. Crematorium staff will assist.
- Coffins normally have six bearers. Ensure that these people are roughly the same height and, if possible, have them practise beforehand. Note: dropping a coffin before or during a funeral is considered one of the worst faux pas one can commit.
- You can have a service in whatever location you wish. At home, a pub, a local hall. You may or may not wish for a religious or non-religious figure to speak.
- In a crematorium try and get the last slot of the day in case things don't go to plan. Or book for an hour. Not everyone need go to the burial site.

✔ **Advantages of DIY funerals.** Cost. The average cost for a so-called 'basic' burial is more than £1,500. A cremation is about £1,200. DIY funerals can be, potentially, free if you are buried in a shroud in your own garden (serious consideration should be given to this option). Dealing with the body can also be helpful in coming to terms with grief.

✘ **Disadvantages of DIY funerals.** Can be messy, stressful and bureaucratic. Could upset more traditional family members. Neighbourly bitching.

Father Kit Cunningham is a Catholic priest

Our lives are a preparation for death. We're not here forever, you know.

Death is very much a part of Catholicism. We're very comfortable with death.

We pray for the dead, unlike the Anglicans. It was only after the Second World War that remembrance became popular. I mean, what could the Anglican Church and government say to those poor mothers to comfort them?

I did a funeral for a 31-year-old New Zealander. He was jogging across the Millennium Bridge in London and simply collapsed and died. It was so sudden that he didn't even instinctively put out a hand to break his fall. At the funeral I had an audience of young people and they were absolutely traumatised. I had never seen a group of young people who looked so vulnerable. I said to them: "I cannot explain it or give you a reason. But I can help you accept it."

You have to accept the inequalities of life. We are not all as pretty or intelligent as each other and we accept that. But we cannot accept the inequality of time!

Anglicans are weedy.

For Catholics, the wake is the time we speak of the person. We celebrate their human side and that is very important.

Memorial services are a bit of a fraud.

One man I know, his father's last wish was to be cremated but the man, his son, refused and had him buried. The man refers to cremation as incineration, which, I think you will agree, is a far harsher term. I don't think anyone will go to Hell by accident, you know. Hitler and Stalin were good candidates for Hell I'd say, although I couldn't possibly say they are definitely there.

What's the phrase? "A Welshman prays on a Sunday and preys on his neighbours the rest of the week." We talk of the practice of faith. That's the key word. Most Anglicans say they are Christian but they don't practise!

I never talk about lapsed Catholics, only resting Catholics. Mostly it's pure laziness, and people feel they are busy all the time. But they are impoverishing their lives! Tell them, tell them!

I'd say the Catholic church is against capital punishment but, on the other hand, it's not a disaster if the person who dies goes to Heaven. It might be early, but it's not a disaster.

You don't have a right to take your own life. But if someone does, they must have had the balance of their mind disturbed. We don't approve, but you must be compassionate.

The sadness of one's life is that one doesn't have the chance to read all the books one wants to.

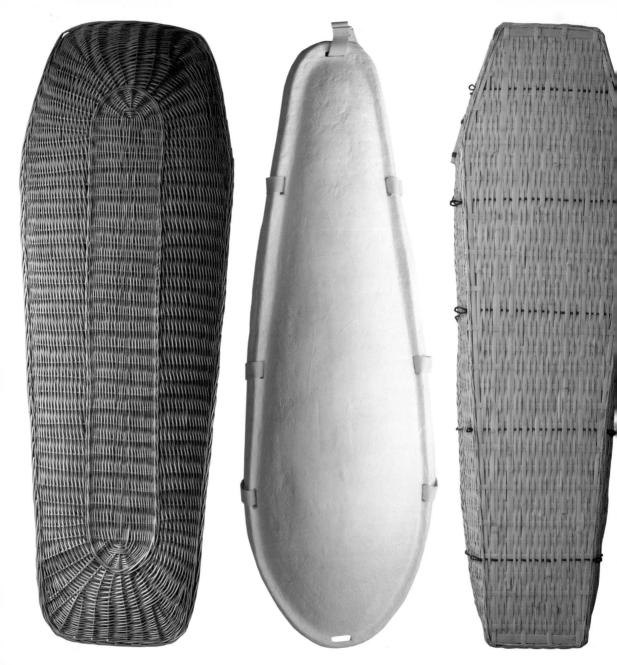

Green funerals

A meadow or woodland burial, an option that is growing in popularity. Memorials and headstones are generally not permitted, but often memorial trees can be planted to mark the grave. For a list of 200-plus natural burial sites, see *The Natural Death Handbook*.

Ecopod coffins are **"for people who want to be buried without damaging the environment".** They are biodegradable, made from recycled newspaper and decorated with paper made from silk and mulberry leaves, with calico mattress and optional feather lining. Cost: £632 (inc VAT and post).

Reuse of graves

The law states that graves can be reused after 50 to 100 years (max), except in the case of war graves. It is estimated that 70 per cent of the public "might be prepared to accept (or at least not object to) the need to reuse graves after an appropriate time", according to an official paper on the subject: *Burial Law and Policy in the 21st Century.*

207

Number of natural burial grounds in the UK.

Coffin types
- Oak, elm, pine.
- Chipboard (non-eco friendly).
- Biodegradable: cardboard, papier mâché, bamboo, willow, "ecopods", wicker, recycled newspaper, seagrass (Australian), biodegradable plastic (German).
- Plastic.
- Zinc or lead-lined (for repatriation).
- Hardwoods (usually US).

DIY pyres

In theory, funeral pyres that cause no "nuisance", that is, no pollution or smell, seem to be legal. Whether they are legal has yet to be tested in the courts. Stephen White, a trustee of the Cremation Society of Great Britain, stresses the need to consult with someone who is insured for giving legal advice, before going ahead.

"I'm planning to be buried in one of the Church of England woodland sites, where I hope to grow into a tree and where one day someone will chop me down and make me into a beautiful piece of furniture." Conservationist David Bellamy.

RIP Bill Annetts (d.1997) **was a former colonel-in-chief of the Sealed Knot, a group that re-enacts battles from the English Civil War. His ashes were shot from a cannon. His widow, Joyce, said: "It's what he wanted."**

Naked

Robert Norton, from Illinois, a committed nudist throughout his life, was denied his final wish – to be buried naked – by his family. The 82-year-old said he wanted to be buried in his birthday suit, but his brother Jack, a minister, said: "He's not going to be buried in the nude." Although Norton did not set out to offend, his insistence on gardening in the nude did upset some neighbours. One, Brenda Loete, admitted she had spent years taking her daughter to the park rather than letting her play in the garden because of the naked old man next door. "We didn't really know him," she said, "we just had him arrested." *Source: BBC.*

Pope's wishes ignored

Catholic Pope John Paul II's final wish, that his private papers be burned, was ignored by his former private secretary. The Pope (d.2005) had asked Archbishop Stanislaw Dziwisz to oversee the burning of his personal documents and notes. "Nothing has been burned," admitted Dziwisz. "Nothing is fit for burning. Everything should be preserved and kept for history, for the future generations – every single sentence. These are great riches that should gradually be made available to the public."

Last wish

Peter Hindley, chief executive of funeral provider Dignity, wants his ashes scattered at sea. **Tony Blackburn**, radio DJ, would like his ashes scattered "all over Radio 1 DJ Sara Cox".

30-40

Average time (in minutes) most crematoriums allocate for a funeral service, although some can be as short as 20 minutes. If concerned, insist on a double session. The cost is minimal and it alleviates the "conveyor-belt" feeling.

We do like to be beside the seaside

Sixteen per cent of people want to have their ashes scattered at sea or on a beach, according to the National Trust Coastal Values Survey. The survey also found 59% have kept something at home that they found on a beach, 49% considered their happiest childhood memory as being by the sea, and 34% often day-dream about being by the sea when going about their everyday life. Seven per cent have proposed on the beach or coastline.

Carl Marlow runs Goasyouplease funerals in Newcastle

The funeral industry is the last closed shop. But it's time it was opened.

I advise people against prepaid funerals. I don't think people should save up to die. People end up saving for the funeral, not heating their house and dying of pneumonia!

I did a lot of mystery shopping before I set up the company. I'd go in to a funeral directors and ask for information about green funerals and cardboard coffins. One woman leaned towards me and whispered: "Don't go for a cardboard coffin, people fall out." No they don't! I was horrified!

A standard coffin costs £70, at most. But the cheapest is about £350.

Funeral directors take the piss. They are charlatans in my eyes. It's not that they are doing anything wrong. But they're not doing anything right, either.

People think an alternative funeral means a wicker coffin. I'd like to see coffins taken to the cemetery in a wheelbarrow. I'd like to see friends of the deceased carry the coffin all the way. Sod the traffic. What are the police going to do? Nothing.

I'd hate to go out in a hearse. The only way you'd get me in one of them was wrapped in a duvet with my feet sticking out the end on show, for shock purposes.

It will cost you £125 for a hearse. A limo will be about £100. Take a cab! It will only cost you a fiver. I always tell families to drive themselves and save their money.

People don't realise that so-called "traditional funerals" were dreamt up by funeral directors. There's no such thing as a traditional funeral. In the past, you'd be left on the kitchen table for a few days and everyone would come round and grieve. Not now. But I see funerals going the same way as weddings.

Flowers are a rip-off. Headstones are a rip-off. A headstone costs, what, £80? They will charge you £600. But most people don't want to know, they don't think about death. They want to get it done as soon as possible and they don't think about the costs.

I mix wild flower seeds in with the ashes. So after they are scattered, there's something to see and you know where the ashes are.

Ignorance is bliss. It must be. Because my head churns.

When my mum died, the funeral director came round and sat down with me, my father and my sister. The funeral director asked about a coffin and I said "the cheapest". My dad hit the roof. We argued, emotions were high. In the end I thought, fine, choose whatever you want, it's your wife. So he goes for the next one up. But you know what? It was the same bastard coffin! I know that now, but who checks?

I believe this is Hell, living. When you die, you're free. That's Utopia. If there was a gun to my head, I'd go for Buddhism.

Ways to go

Up, up and away

Jim McTaggart, a Scottish pilot, has devised a method of firing ashes out of his light aircraft using a high-pressure system. Previously, because of air pressures, the cremated remains tended to be sucked back into an aircraft. The Edinburgh-based pilot charges £650, depending on distance flown, based on two hours' flying in his 1930s-style bi-plane.

The final frontier

US-based Space Services Inc. fires ashes into space. Costs vary. To fire off one gram of the remains costs about $1,000. For seven grams, it's $5,300. Star Trek creator Gene Roddenberry and 1960s pop icon Dr Timothy Leary were fired into space in 1997.

Moon funeral (low turnout, no atmosphere)

Dr Eugene Shoemaker, a US scientific historian "who almost single-handedly created planetary science as a discipline distinct from astronomy", with the help of NASA, had his cremated remains placed on the surface of the moon.

Become a star?

There are commercial services that offer to register a star name and issue a certificate on a person's behalf for a fee. Don't do it. The only official body that can give names to stars and other astronomical objects is the International Astronomical Union. It does not register star names for any individual, other than the astronomer who discovers it.

Diamond geezer?

LifeGem, a US-based company, creates "high-quality diamonds" from cremated ashes. Diamonds can be between .25 carat and 1.0 carat. More than 100 diamonds can be created from one person, and pets can be done too. Prices range from £2,250 to £11,950 per diamond. Pets and people cost the same since the company "only takes a maximum of 200 grams of ash".

> ## "On 6 February, 1771, Colonel Luttrell arrived at a masquerade ball dressed as a coffin,"
>
> according to Dr Julian Litten in his book *The English Way of Death*. "Someone present at the event said that Luttrell cast such a 'pall of gloom' over the proceedings that he was obliged to leave almost as soon as he arrived."

RIP **Alistair Cooke (d.2004): The broadcaster and journalist wanted his ashes scattered in New York's Central Park, but local authorities do not allow the disposal of human remains in its parks. His daughter got around the problem by putting the ashes into Starbucks cups, walking into the park, and scattering his ashes on the grass. Note: it has since been alleged that some of Cooke's bones were stolen prior to cremation.**

102mph

Speed at which a Gosport-based funeral director was driving his hearse when arrested in 1984.

Naming planets

Mercury, Venus, Mars, Jupiter, and Saturn were named by the Roman after their Gods.

Mercury: There are Tolstoy (d1910) and Bach (d.1750) craters on planet Mercury, and the Wagner (d.1884) Mountain.

Moon: Craters on the moon are named after people. Examples include Socrates (d.399BC?), Plato (d.347BC), Archimedes (d.211BC?), Tsiolkovsky (d.1935), Pasteur (d.1895) and Kuiper (d.1973).

Venus: With one exception (the Maxwell mountains named after the 19th century physicist James Clerk Maxwell (d.1879), all features on planet Venus are named after famous women, including the Sacagawea (d.1812?) crater, the Florence Nightingale (d.1910) channel and the Cleopatra (d30BC?) crater.

Saturn: Many features on Saturn's moon Mimas are named after characters in King Arthur's court, including Galahad, Lancelot, Kay and Guenevere craters. Many features on the moon Enceladus are named after characters in the Arabian Nights, including Aladdin, Ali Baba and Sinbad.

"When anyone asks me how I can best describe my experience in nearly 40 years at sea, I merely say, uneventful... I have never been in any accident... I never saw a wreck and never have been wrecked nor was I ever in any predicament that threatened to end in disaster of any sort." **Captain of the Titanic, Edward Smith**

The supposedly unsinkable largest ever passenger liner did just that on 15 April 1912. Altogether 1,513 people died, out of a total of 2,224. Ninety-four per cent of women and children in first class survived, compared with 81 per cent of those in second class and 47 per cent in third class. Also lost on that day were 3,364 bags of mail, a Renault car, five grand pianos and four cases of opium.

Sue Harvey is a funeral director for Dignity

I don't do miserable.

I've always wanted to do this job, from about the age of eight. I loved wearing black and sitting around in cemeteries. They're so peaceful.

My dad doesn't really let me discuss what I do, my mum thinks it's fantastic, my partner shocks people by telling them. My three children tell their friends I'm a secretary and tell me not to come and pick them up from school in my uniform.

People do say things to me because I am a woman. You hear rumours. The pallbearers, some funeral directors. I have to try extra hard and show that I'm as good as a bloke. Actually, I have to pretend to be one of the lads. It's sad really. One old bloke always says to me: "What are you going to fuck up today, then?"

My saddest time is when someone comes in and the person they have lived together with for the past 40-50 years has gone. That's really hard.

You have to shut yourself off from it, but I do cry. I can be stood at the back of a church and in floods of tears.

I did one funeral where one half of the family was threatening to kill the other half. There had been bricks through windows, verbal threats. I had to have minders with me just in case anything kicked off. But it all passed off peacefully. Families are often at loggerheads, arguing about the cost of the coffin, either too much or too little.

When they come to see us, people are often on the edge. One wrong word can be enough. So we avoid the word "dead" and "body" and "corpse". We don't say "died", we say "passed away". And we never say "good morning" or "good afternoon" when we answer the phone. It's obviously not that good if you're phoning us.

There are a lot of myths around dying. I think doing this job has taken away the fear.

I don't think there's life after death.

I'm terrible with names. Faces I can do.

One man called me in the middle of the night, two o'clock I think it was, and announced that his wife had died. I'd only just opened my eyes and said "I'm sorry". "Not half as sorry as I am," he snapped back. I was mortified. What do you say to that?

A funeral will cost between £1,700 and up to about £4,000. One lady spent £20,000 on a coffin for her son. She said since she'd never get the chance to buy him his first car or help him buy a house she would spend the money on a nice coffin.

You have dreams. Mine's that I'm in a coffin going into an incinerator. The coffin stops and I'm screaming, but the man can't hear me...

£1bn

What the British funeral business is worth annually. There are about 2,500 funeral directors in Britain.

How much?

The cost of funerals has risen way above the rate of inflation. A recent survey discovered that nearly half of all burials cost more than £2,000.

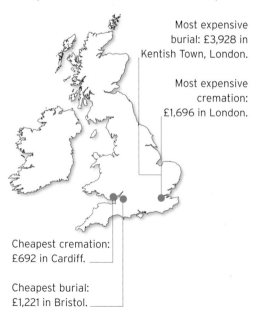

Most expensive burial: £3,928 in Kentish Town, London.

Most expensive cremation: £1,696 in London.

Cheapest cremation: £692 in Cardiff.

Cheapest burial: £1,221 in Bristol.

Sharing

Local parishes in England used to own a "parish coffin" for members of the community to share. Bodies were placed in the ground in a shroud. Possessing a coffin of your own was an unattainable luxury for the majority of people in the 16th century.

Cremated remains weigh roughly 2kg (5-7lb).

How to scatter ashes: a guide

1   Choose a suitable location.
2   Check the wind direction.
3   The entire scattering party should stand upwind.
4   Scatter accordingly.
    If scattering over a grassy or woodland area, flower seeds can be added. This will help you remember where you scattered the ashes if you come back.

Full time?

About 30 per cent of the population still choose to be buried in traditional churchyards and municipal cemeteries, meaning churches and cemeteries must find room for 160,000 new plots each year. Many metropolitan graveyards or cemeteries are already full. Most burial plots are sold on a system of leasehold.

The Rt. Hon. The Earl Grey, **elected 1992,**
is president of The Cremation Society
of Great Britain. The 6th Earl, he is also
chairman of the London Cremation Company,
a former member of the Select Committee
on Consolidation of Bills and former Liberal
Democrat party spokesman on social services.

25,000
Estimated number of burial grounds in the UK.

600,000
The annual death rate. It will rise by just two per
cent by 2006, still four per cent below the level
recorded a decade earlier in 1996.

Biggest cemetery (hardest to find)
Brookwood, Surrey, formerly called the London
Necropolis. The biggest cemetery in the world
when opened in 1854, it even had a station

5% club: Seventy per cent of
the population opt for cremation. This is the
practice of disposing of a corpse by burning.
This often takes place in a crematorium or
crematory. The body is placed in a wooden box
and burnt at a temperature of 1,400° to 2,100°
Fahrenheit (760° to 1,150° Celsius). The remains
consist of about five per cent of the body's
original mass. There are 250 crematoria in the
UK and estimates put the number of cremations
(to date) in the UK at more than 20 million.

built on the site so that the funeral trains from
Waterloo station could drop off funeral parties
and coffins. There used to be a sign above the
bar in the Brookwood Cemetery station that
read: "Spirits served here." The St Edward
Brotherhood live on the site. That said, it's
difficult to locate the massive site, "home" to
240,000 souls, as there are remarkably few signs
locally. London parishes that use Brookwood
Cemetery: Bermondsey; St George's; Bloomsbury;
Chelsea; St Paul's; and Deptford.

"Beneath lies buried the founder of this church and city,
Christopher Wren, who lived more then 90 years, not for
himself but for the public good. Reader, if you seek his
monument, look around you." Christopher Wren's epitaph in St Paul's Cathedral.

Gary Doswell and wife Beryl are freelance gravediggers

When you backfill a grave, you have to get back in the hole to tread it down so it's all even. Well, that can be a bit of a nightmare when some of the family come back 20 minutes later and you're up to your waist in their relation's grave stamping up and down.

We get totally ignored by some people. Then again, others offer us tea and toast. We even had the offer of Pimms at one funeral. Some people have a picnic at the graveside.

A handful of joints, cans of beer, bottles of wine. People throw all sorts into a grave. One lot of mourners poured a bottle of champagne in and at another funeral a man poured in a pint of Guinness. We even had one funeral where some bloke poured in a bag of white powder, which was ironic since the guy had died of an overdose.

At Rye harbour the graveyard is by the sea, so you're literally digging through the beach. They only do single-depth graves there. Rain and water are our biggest problems.

Being outside all day is great. You see all sorts of nature and you get to see the seasons. Even the cold fresh mornings are nice. The ground doesn't freeze in winter though. I mean, we're not in the arctic! The top layer may be frosty but that's about it.

Once we've dug the hole, we go and sit in the van. I did one where I parked the van too close to the funeral. There was a lot of wailing and crying and I admit that was upsetting.

We dig up a lot of clay pipes. We've come across horseshoes four foot underground in ground supposedly untouched. We've found strange pennies, a Turkish one and a Chinese one once. I don't know how they got there. We find a lot of bucket handles as well.

Buried? No. I want to be freeze-dried.

People are superstitious. I remember we were supposed to dig one hole but it was plot number 666 and no one would take it. They changed the plot number to 667.

Do we ever get spooked? Sometimes. Some of the headstones are granite and the torchlight reflects back to you. That can be a bit of a shock.

This job has shown me that so-called Christians are not as Christian as they like to think. We'll be in a churchyard digging a hole all day sometimes and they won't let us use the toilet! The people with the key, usually some old girl, won't let us in when I know full well there's a toilet in there. That's a bugbear of mine.

I've got a lot of shovels but they don't last. They split and break. Even the well-known and supposedly good brands. I thought about going to one of them for sponsorship.

Burial at sea

You need a free licence from the Department for Environment, Food and Rural Affairs (Defra) for burial at sea. There are only 20-50 burials at sea each year, not least because Defra has produced a minefield of bureaucratic guidelines to discourage it. The boat must be skippered by a captain with a Yacht Master's Certificate. Embalmed bodies are not permitted to be buried at sea. Cost: up to £4,000 if organised by a funeral director, less if privately organised.

Potential problems of burial at sea
- Costs.
- Weather.
- Limited number of guests.
- Bodies washing up on shore.
- Fishing vessels trawling the bodies up.
- Seasickness (of the living).
- Shipwreck.

Burial at sea: coffin specification
All corners of the coffin should be butt-jointed.

Forty to 50 holes of 50mm (2in) should be drilled into the coffin. To ensure that the body remains on the seabed it is required that approximately 200kg of iron, steel or concrete should be clamped to the base of the coffin.
Source: Food and Environment Protection Act 1985: Burial at Sea.

There are three places to be buried at sea around the English coastline.

An area nine miles from the mouth of the river Tyne.

Near Newhaven, Sussex

The Needles Spoil Ground, to the west of the Isle of Wight

"A band of plastic or other durable material should be locked around the neck of the deceased and this band should be either punch-marked or indelibly marked with a telephone number and reference number that would allow the remains to be positively identified should the need arise."
Source: Food and Environment Protection Act 1985: Burial at Sea.

Cemetery *n.* the public cemetery originated in the Victorian period. Under common law, every parishioner and inhabitant of a parish had a right to be buried in his or her parish churchyard or burial ground.

£100–£1,000

Costs for burial vary widely throughout the UK, according to the Environment, Transport and Regional Affairs Select Committee. This does "not represent good value for UK citizens", the report says.

Manchester City Council "rules in cemeteries and crematoria"

- The playing of radios and similar equipment is forbidden at all times.
- It is an offence for visitors to bring in bicycles, scooters, mopeds or motorcycles into a cemetery.
- Smoking is prohibited in cemeteries near any place where a funeral or religious service is taking place.
- The use of still, cine and television cameras is strictly prohibited at or near any grave before, during or after an interment.

City of London Cemetery and Crematorium, Newham, Essex. Considered one of the "best" cemeteries in the country, the 200-acre site near Epping Forest was purchased by the Corporation of London in 1854. The cost (in 2004) for a "vault, fully-constructed 9' x 4'6" (plus landing for full memorial) stood at a whopping £26,950.

No body shall be buried in such a manner that any part of the coffin is less than three feet below the level of any ground adjoining the grave

According to the Local Authorities' Cemeteries Order 1977.

The "Highgate of the North", Newcastle's Jesmond Old Cemetery was opened in 1836. Buried within the grounds are John Woodger (inventor of the curing process for kippers), several Chinese sailors and a 28-year-old Algerian dancer Zaza Ben-I-Ford, who took part in the 1929 North East Coast Exhibition. Good for walking in. Since 1836, 25,000 people have been buried here.

Penny Black (left)
is a Buddhist.
Her sister-in-law,
Caroline Black,
is a Humanist
officiant

Penny Black is a Buddhist

I hit a low point in my life in a phone box on Marylebone High Street in London. I stepped out of the phone box and thought I could either turn left and throw myself under a passing bus or go back in the phone box and call someone I knew who could help me. He was a Buddhist and that's how I got into it.

I practise the same sort of Buddhism that Tina Turner does. We follow the Lotus Sutra. We chant, twice a day, in the morning and the evening. It's the sound of the universe.

We believe there is only one fear, the fear of death.

When you die you don't go anywhere. Heaven and Hell are where you are. They are inside everyone. When you are alive, you're like an iceberg. You came out of the water and when you die you become part of the water again.

We call reincarnation the eternity of life but people think it's all about coming back as a dog. That's not the point. We believe there is life elsewhere in the universe so you could come back at any time anywhere in the universe.

We're not like Catholics who can get to the end of their lives, ask for forgiveness, and everything is okay. Lots of Italians are Buddhists.

We respect life, but I do eat meat. You shouldn't kill a wasp but you can't drive yourself mad with it.

Buddhists have never been on *Thought for the Day*.

I used to live in Austria. I went there to learn German when I was 17 and I never wanted to come back. After six years though, I missed the English sense of humour – and English men. Did you know, lorries can't be driven at the weekend in Austria?

People say Buddhist funerals are happy occasions. But that's like saying going through labour doesn't hurt. It's bollocks.

Buddhists don't carry donor cards.

If you have six months to live, the point is you could do something with those six months. So we're against euthanasia.

Suicide is a moment of despair. It has the most awful effect on everyone around them.

My family thought I'd grow out of Buddhism. Now I think they feel it's done me good. My father was in hospital having an operation on his back and I chanted for him. I think he really appreciated that.

The main misconceptions? People ask why my head isn't shaven, why I don't wear orange robes, if they will come back as a dog, if I'm a vegetarian and wonder why I'm not calmer.

If you don't believe in anything, what do you believe in?

Caroline Black is a Humanist officiant

I did a gangster's funeral. I didn't know he was a gangster. He'd been married three times and his second wife organised the funeral. On the day, I arrived early and was told there was someone waiting for me. It was a small lady with bleach-blonde hair; it was his daughter. She announced: "I'm his next-of-kin, not that effing bitch. This is the music we're having and I'm going to say something." When everyone else arrived, I told the second wife about the daughter. "That bitch!" she shrieked, and the two of them had a full-on fist fight. I had to hold them apart. It turns out he was an armed robber. Anyway, at the end of the service, one of the grandchildren asked me if granddad was going to Hell! **Humanists are anarchists. They are extreme atheists.**

I got obsessed with Jesus for a while when I was an adolescent. I think it was around the time of *Jesus Christ Superstar*, but university ended that.

I've done a lot of funerals for lapsed Jewish people.

I was interviewed by John Peel on *Home Truths*. It was because I kept my dad's ashes in the wardrobe for 11 years. I used to get him out on New Year's Eve and take him down the pub.

My friend died with his hand in mine. He'd been diagnosed with pancreatic cancer and for his last few days, he stayed at our house. We were listening to Miles Davis at the time. It was his favourite. It was as if an electric impulse passed through him, down his arm and across his body. That was it. I remember being absolutely gobsmacked. I said to him: "You're not there, are you?" I said it two or three times, then went downstairs and burst into tears. I had to go back up and check. I asked him again if he'd died. I did his funeral.

Is there an answer to life after death? Humanists would say that there is. You're dead, and that's it. I find it consoling to think that there is no parallel universe.

My mother had a stroke and went to hospital. I resigned from my job to look after her at home when she came out. My husband and I altered the house to make room for the wheelchair. We even widened the drive. Once we'd made the alterations and everything was ready, just before she was due to come out, she died.

We're not in the business of tea and hankies. Empathy is the key thing.

One funeral had that cricket commentary played at the service. The one where Jonathan Agnew and Brian Johnstone can't stop giggling. *The Bright Side of Life*, we've had, and *Bring Me Sunshine*.

People are realising that Christian services aren't satisfying. If you never go to church, why have a church service when you die?

Did you know that roses like the alkaline in bones? That's why when you scatter ashes in a graveyard or at a crematorium it's often onto roses.

I did the funeral for Nelson Mandela's dentist.

115

"At Diana, Princess of Wales's funeral, they laid on extra trains for people to come up to London. My sister slept overnight. I got the 5.30am train up. It was the biggest funeral since Churchill and her brother's speech was very moving. Everyone went up hoping for mass booing of the Duke of Edinburgh. It was a strange occasion, but everyone was friendly." John Clarke, author of *The Brookwood Necropolis Railway*.

3 million

Number of mourners who lined the route of the funeral procession of Diana, Princess of Wales. More than one million bouquets were left at her London home, Kensington Palace. Famous mourners included Sir Elton John, Tom Cruise, Steven Spielberg, Sir Richard Branson.

17%

The rise in the overall suicide rate in England and Wales during the four weeks following Diana's funeral, compared with the average reported for that period in the four previous years, according to a report, *Effect of death of Diana, Princess of Wales on suicide and deliberate self-harm*, published in the *British Journal of Psychiatry*.

Rebellion
Carlisle cemetery opened the first woodland burial site in the UK where, instead of headstones, the dead can opt to have a tree planted. Because of its location, Carlisle has always been a place of rebellion and the cemetery reflects that. There are Unitarians, Quakers and Communists buried here.

Blake, Bunyan and Defoe
Bunhill Fields burial ground (Bunhill originally meant Bone Hill) is just off the City Road in London. William Blake (d.1827) is buried here as are John Bunyan (d.1688) and Daniel Defoe (d.1731). Golders Green Crematorium is on Hoop Lane, London. Directly opposite is a Jewish cemetery, the odd thing about it being that all the gravestones are flat.

How to be buried at Westminster Abbey
The Dean of Westminster must give his

permission for all burials and monuments in the Abbey. Only ashes are permitted. People who have served the Abbey in an official capacity, such as a dean, a canon, organist or "Surveyor to the Fabric" may be buried here and "eminent persons of British nationality" from various fields may be considered. The last poet interred was John Masefield in 1967, and Sir Laurence Olivier, actor, was buried here in 1991. Famous poets or writers buried in Westminster Abbey include Charles Dickens, Alfred Lord Tennyson and Rudyard Kipling. Elizabethan poet Ben Jonson (d.1637) is supposedly buried standing upright.

The churchyard of St Martin-in-the-Fields, London, was only 200ft (60m) square yet, in the early 1840s, it was estimated to contain the remains of between 60,000 and 70,000 people.

"Nearer, my God, to thee." The song famously played by the ship's band aboard the *Titanic* as it sank in 1912.

Plymouth's frequent visitor
A quarter of a million people are buried at Ford Park Cemetery in Plymouth. It received several direct hits during the Blitz. Sydney Douglas Potter, "a frequent visitor" to the cemetery, left it more than £200,000 in his Will in 2004.

Who is the Unknown Warrior?
Bodies of British soldiers were exhumed from four main First World War battle areas, the Aisne, the Somme, Ypres and Arras, on the night of 7 November 1920. Each body was covered with a Union Jack and placed on a stretcher. The officer in charge, Brigadier-General LJ Wyatt, was blindfolded and then pointed to one of the bodies. It was placed in a coffin and the remaining three bodies were removed and reburied.

The following day the body was taken to Boulogne under escort where it was placed in a coffin made of English oak. British troops then took over guard duties and the body crossed the English Channel in the destroyer Verdun, receiving a Field Marshal's 19-gun salute on arrival at Dover. Crowds gathered at every station on the way as the Unknown Warrior's train travelled north from the Kent coat to London's Victoria station.

The grave, which contains soil from France, is covered by a slab of black Belgian marble from a quarry near Namur. See it at Westminster Abbey, London.

John Harris runs T Crib & Son in London's East End

It was never a great bird-puller at school. It tended to stop people in their tracks. I wanted to be a vet or an accountant, but you get sucked into this business, like a vacuum.

Drink and this profession go hand in hand. I think in the past it was worse. You'd go to a house and, as funeral director, be offered a drink. If you're doing five funerals a day, it mounts up.

My earliest memories of the business? The smell of the polish.

When I first took over we could go for weeks without a funeral. But then we did 60 in a week once. Mind you that was mayhem.

Not everyone wants cheap-and-cheerful. We did the funeral of a publican. He had 22 limos, three hearses and you've never seen so many flowers.

We did a funeral for a gypsy family. Two gypsy men, the sons, arrived in a police van, handcuffed to prison warders. The place was crawling with police but there must have been a thousand gypsies there. Before you know it, the bolt-cutters were out, snip, and the two men were off. Although there was a lot of police, there weren't that many and they're not stupid. The gypsies closed ranks and that was that!

There were three daughters and a son in this house and the son was a bit loose. My brother Graham went round to organise the funeral for their mother. Anyway, the lad wanted a piper at the funeral but the girls said no. Next thing you know, he's getting agitated and heads to the kitchen when they hear a drawer opening. The girls shout: "He's got a knife, quick, out the window!" Graham was the first one out.

We were at the City of London Cemetery and had to release two doves. So as they've gone up, out of nowhere, this sparrowhawk slams into one of them and kills it. You shouldn't laugh but I think even the family found that funny. At another one, the family wanted each of the 12 grandchildren to release a dove. So the first one throws the first dove up and on it went up the line. Anyway, about halfway up the line, one girl throws hers up and it comes straight back down again and hits the ground with a thud. She was holding the thing so tight she'd accidentally killed it!

A funeral is a thanksgiving service for a person's life. It's not about readings from *Corinthians*.

There's no funeral museum in this country and that's what I'm trying to set up. But not as a peep show. It's about education, about life, about the social history of this country.

Woodland burial is niche. It's a bit middle class for around here. I'd say it's about 0.1 per cent of our business. People aren't too environmentally friendly round here.

I'd like to think there would be a big turnout for my funeral but I haven't really thought about it. It doesn't matter that I work in the business. I mean, I'm not immune from grief.

My uncle had a motto: "You're a long time dead." You've got to get on with life.

Barry Marchant is head of operations at Co-operative Funeralcare

People write to us wanting us to confirm that their loved one is dead. I think that's come out of the Shipman case. I can assure people that after embalming the person is dead. The number of people who get embalmed is quite high, actually.

If you're bereaved, you want to speak to someone who has had life experience, not an 18-year-old.

I remember when funeral directors had grim shopfronts, dirty curtains, maybe a map in the window and, if you're lucky, an old picture of a horse-drawn cart. And they had the cheek to call them funeral homes! We're trying to take the fear out of funeral directors, trying to modernise them.

There used to be 650,000 funerals a year, but now it's more like 523,000.

Why purple? It's not purple, it's lilac! We did 18 months of research to come up with lilac. We wanted to get away from black and gold but remain respectful. Some colours can't be worn in certain churches.

Many people look back on the funeral of a loved one and wish they could have done more. We call that the secret disappointment. People wish they'd chosen different music, perhaps taken the cortege past one of the deceased's old haunts, or had them dressed in their favourite clothes.

My nan is 88. She doesn't stop talking about her funeral. I think it gives her peace of mind.

I'm always asked two questions. Do they really burn the coffin? And are the ashes really the ashes? The answer is yes to both.

This job has helped me come to terms with death. It's taught me that the body of the deceased is the shell of the person. That's my personal belief.

People don't know what to do with the ashes. It's a big dilemma. One thing you could do is place them in an urn and build it into a bird bath.

Funeral directors do gossip about each other, but never about clients.

I definitely want to be cremated.

One florist was asked to make a bouquet in the shape of a six-foot joint. Another funeral wanted an arrangement of vegetables on the coffin instead of flowers. Anything's possible.

Ninety per cent of funeral directors have a funeral service in their pockets in case the vicar doesn't turn up.

One man's last wish was to have his ashes scattered around the world by his wife. It encouraged her to travel and see the world even after her husband's death.

Beware of Wills. They are often read after the funeral but may specify aspects of the funeral.

Random costs of burial

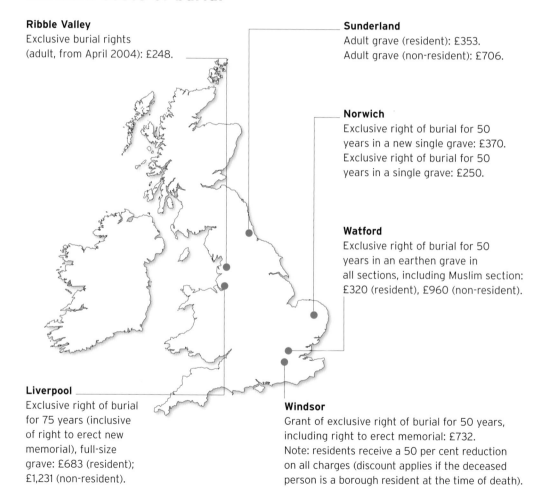

Ribble Valley
Exclusive burial rights
(adult, from April 2004): £248.

Sunderland
Adult grave (resident): £353.
Adult grave (non-resident): £706.

Norwich
Exclusive right of burial for 50
years in a new single grave: £370.
Exclusive right of burial for 50
years in a single grave: £250.

Watford
Exclusive right of burial for 50
years in an earthen grave in
all sections, including Muslim section:
£320 (resident), £960 (non-resident).

Liverpool
Exclusive right of burial
for 75 years (inclusive
of right to erect new
memorial), full-size
grave: £683 (resident);
£1,231 (non-resident).

Windsor
Grant of exclusive right of burial for 50 years,
including right to erect memorial: £732.
Note: residents receive a 50 per cent reduction
on all charges (discount applies if the deceased
person is a borough resident at the time of death).

It was custom in the Royal Navy to sew up a corpse into his hammock before dropping it in the sea. The sailmaker always put the last stitch through the nose of the corpse to ensure the person was dead.

Soar point

The River Soar in Leicestershire is officially approved as the "Ganges" where British Hindus and Sikhs can scatter the ashes of their dead, instead of flying to India to perform the last rites. The Environment Agency has authorised a section of the river to be used for the purpose after requests from the local Asian community. Shastriji Prakashbhai Pandya, a Hindu priest who officiates at the ceremonies, said: "When I close my eyes, this could be the Ganges."

3,000

Number of people thought to be buried in Westminster Abbey. The precise number is unknown since no formal register was kept until 1607. This figure does not include the many monks who were buried here up to 1540. The Abbey contains more than 800 inscribed gravestones, tombs, monuments and memorial stones.

John O'Groats

Scotland has two locations where it is possible to have a burial at sea: 210 nautical miles due west of Oban and 15 nautical miles due west of John O'Groats.

Bradford

Undercliffe Cemetery has "possibly the finest collection of Victorian funerary art in the North of England" and overlooks the city of Bradford and the Yorkshire Dales. It covers more than 25 acres and contains more than 23,000 graves.

The largest cemetery in the world is Rookwood, in Australia. In terms of the largest number of graves, that grim distinction goes to the Piskariovskoye cemetery, St Petersburg.

"I wish peace and affluence to all my friends and a piece of effluence to all my enemies"

Last Will and Testament, Anon

What now for the living?

DEAD AHEAD

> **"Epitaph:** An inscription on a tomb showing that virtues acquired by death have a retroactive effect."
>
> Ambrose Bierce (d.1914) *The Devil's Dictionary*

"I am ready to meet my Maker. Whether my Maker is prepared for the great ordeal of meeting me is another matter."

Epitaph, Winston Churchill (d.1965)

"A master of comedy his genius in the art of humour brought gladness to the world he loved."

Epitaph, Stan Laurel (d.1969)

"Workers of all lands unite. The philosophers have only interpreted the world in various ways; the point is to change it."

Epitaph, Karl Marx (d.1883)

"He fell off his dog-cart."

Epitaph, Reuben Henry Williams (d.1884), buried in Nunhead Cemetery, London.

"Alien tears will fill for him Pity's long-broken urn, For mourners will be outcast men And outcasts always mourn"

Epitaph, Oscar Wilde (d.1900)

"Say not in grief 'he is no more' but live in thankfulness that he was"

Hebrew proverb

"What the caterpillar perceives is the end, to the butterfly is just the beginning."

Richard Bach

"A tomb now suffices for him for whom the world was not enough"

Alexander the Great (d. AD323)

Untitled

Do not stand at my grave and weep;
I am not there. I do not sleep.
I am a thousand winds that blow.
I am the diamond glints on snow.
I am the sunlight on ripened grain.
I am the gentle autumn's rain.
When you awaken in the morning's hush,
I am the swift uplifting rush
of quiet birds in circled flight.
I am the soft stars that shine at night.
Do not stand at my grave and cry;
I am not there, I did not die.

Mary Elizabeth Frye (d.2004)

"As the flowers are all
made sweeter by the
sunshine and the dew,
So this old world is made
brighter by the lives
Of folks like you"

Bonnie Parker (d.1934)

"TANDEM FELIX"
(Happy at last)

Gustavus III, King of Sweden (d.1792)

"If I should die,
think only this of me:
That there's some corner
of a foreign field
That is for ever England."

Brooke, Rupert (d.1915)

"A Genius of Comedy
His Talent Brought Joy and
Laughter to All the World."

Oliver Hardy (d.1956)

"She did it the hard way"

Bette Davis (d.1989)

"The best is yet to come"

Frank Sinatra (d.1998)

"A Gentle Man and
a Gentleman"

Jack Dempsey (d.1983)

April Plant is a barrister

The worst parts of human nature come out in Wills. A solicitor friend of mine told me that the son was on the phone after his mother's death asking what he'd get. That in itself is not unusual, but the mother had only been dead 15 minutes. Fifteen minutes!

It's a misconception that you must do everything stipulated in a Will.

If a relative cannot be found, the money goes to the Government. If you live in the north, the money ends up with the Duchy of Lancaster. In other words, the Queen.

Most problems I see are because people try and do their own Wills. But legal language is very specific. It's no good reading an article in *Marie Claire* and thinking you can do it.

Doing a Will shouldn't cost much more than £75. It's about £100 for a husband and wife. Banks do Wills and they are very good, actually. More expensive, perhaps, but they are better at administering an estate. I'd much rather deal with a bank than a solicitor.

An old man died in Birmingham. As executor, I went to people's houses and would be the first one to do so after the death. The flat was immaculate. It didn't have a lot of furniture and what was there was old. He kept his mother's room exactly as it had been when she died 30 years previously. Anyway, the first thing you do in these situations is to clear out the perishable food, but there was no food, just some baked beans and a packet of biscuits. I found a receipt for his weekly shopping and it was for £8. So I loaded all the paperwork I could find into a bin bag and took it home to work out if he had any money or accounts. I found lots of share certificates and it turns out he used to play the stock markets. He was worth £800,000.

One woman left all her money to a charity and nothing to her husband. She explained in her Will that, 40 years earlier, when her mother had visited once, her husband had said something like 'when's that old bat going?' and she'd never forgiven him. He was mortified.

Probate is so underregulated it's amazing and there's a lot of fraud. I could tell you 20 ways to commit probate fraud but I'm not going to.

If you walk into a property in which someone has died, here are some tips. Open the door and let some air in. Don't march straight in or you'll be marching straight out again being sick. Once you're in, take three or four deep breaths of air in through your mouth. Then you'll be fine. Well, it worked for me. In those situations, the smell is indescribable, but unique. Like an elephant.

I know what I want for my funeral, the best party ever! I want to be buried in my village churchyard. I've told my mum that, but I suppose if we both died at the same time, then no one else would know.

Actually, I don't have a Will.

Taxing the dead

Death duties were introduced into Britain in 1694. The taxation of inheritance dates back to Roman times and has, to this day, never been enthusiastically embraced.

What is cloning?

Copying a biological entity (a gene or organism or cell) and reproducing it. There are different types of cloning: DNA, reproductive and therapeutic.

Only one in three adults has a Will. A Will through a solicitor will cost about £45.

RIP **Dolly the sheep** (d.2003). **Born on 5 July 1996, Dolly was the first mammal cloned from an adult cell. Suffering from a progressive lung disease, Dolly was "euthanased" on St Valentine's Day. Sheep can live up the age of 16. More than 90% of cloning attempts fail to produce viable offspring.**

Six simple steps before you make a Will

1 List all the items you have to leave, including, for example, house and contents, cars, savings, accounts, and note their rough value.

2 Consider who you would like to provide for and in what way. Write down the full names, including middle names, and the addresses of all such people and the dates of birth of all children to be named in the Will.

3 Consider whether you would like to leave money or property "in trust" for children or grandchildren until they are grown up, and at what age you think they should inherit your gift.

4 Decide who you would like to receive your sentimental belongings.

5 Consider whether you would like to leave money to charity (bequests to charities are not liable to inheritance tax).

6 Choose one or more executors to wind up your affairs. They can be spouses, children, members of the family or friends. Get their agreement in advance if possible. If whoever is chosen finds the task too onerous, a solicitor can take over.

"Don't say you don't have enough time. You have exactly the same number of hours per day that were given to Helen Keller, Pasteur, Michelangelo, Mother Teresa, Leonardo da Vinci, Thomas Jefferson and Albert Einstein." H Jackson Brown.

Inheritance tax

"A voluntary tax, paid only by those who distrust their heirs more than they dislike the Inland Revenue."

Roy Jenkins.

£263,000

The minimum value at which estates are liable for 40% inheritance tax. The threshold will rise by £12,000 to £275,000 in the 2005-06 tax year (a rise of 5.7%). It will then climb to £285,000 in 2006-07 (up 3.6%) and to £300,000 in 2007-08 (a further 5.2% rise).

Dead head

When it comes to cryogenic preservation, brains are cooled to minus 196°C, the temperature of liquid nitrogen, for long-term storage. During the 1980s, the goal shifted from whole-body to brain-only or "neuro-preservation", on the assumption that the rest of the body could be re-grown, perhaps by the cloning of the person's DNA. Although legally dead, cryonicists call a preserved person a "patient" rather than a "corpse".

Body to science

People who wish to leave their bodies for medical education or research should make arrangements before they die and inform their next of kin. On death the relatives should contact HM Inspector of Anatomy who will advise on what should be done. Upon acceptance the medical school will arrange for eventual cremation or burial. (Note: non-cancerous bodies are preferred). For more information, visit www.dh.gov.uk.

Safe-keeping

You can save a copy of your Will at the Principal Probate Registry, based in London. Call it on 020 7947 7022 and you will be sent an envelope to send it in. The service costs £5.

Free will

The Institute of Cancer Research runs a scheme under which solicitors write Wills for people over the age of 50 without charge. The Institute pays, hoping the individual will mention it in the Will. Note: there is no obligation to do so.

Sneaky last wish

If wishing for something unusual in your Will, which your beneficiaries could obstruct, such as a garden burial, you could make all gifts to them in the Will conditional on the request being carried out.

Joyce and Ivan Fox work at Crazy Coffins

We made one wooden coffin in the shape of an egg. The lady who requested it wants to be buried in the foetal position. We did another in the shape of an electric guitar.

I was interviewed for Kiss 100 FM once. Should I tell you this? Well, someone called in and asked if we could do one in the shape of Kylie Minogue. He said it would be the only chance he'd have to get inside her!

We have a French artist that draws on the coffins. She's trying to set up a coffin exhibition in Paris but it's not easy. The French are very conservative.

We had one lady ask about doing a Mosquito coffin. The First World War aeroplane, not the insect.

Tradition is going by the board. People aren't going to church and I think that may be one reason this sort of thing is becoming more acceptable. When you think of the funeral service itself, with all the talk of dust to dust, ashes to ashes, well, few people actually believe it. People like a bit of theatre.

We scattered my mother's ashes in a Scottish river. I remember we all had to clamber over a fence that had a warning sign on it saying no trespassing. We then had to scramble down a ravine. The funeral director nearly fell down it. He was only saved when my sister grabbed onto his coat-tails.

One person called and asked if we'd do an Angel of the North coffin. There's a lady in Leicestershire who has commissioned a coffin in the shape of a ballet shoe. The danger with these coffins is people thinking we're not being respectful. It's a grave subject in every sense.

We went to a Greek funeral a few years ago. The men don't shave for 40 days and they stop all the clocks. Everybody must kiss the coffin. After it is lowered into the ground and handfuls of soil are thrown on top, they break bread over the grave, eat it and drink wine. It was lovely. And there were children there, which is important. I found the funeral very satisfying, very upbeat.

When I was young, children were shielded from death. I was told my grandmother had died but that was all. It was like she'd vanished off the map. Heaven forbid something terrible might happen, like you show your emotions.

When Diana died there was mass hysteria, completely out of proportion. I mean, they didn't actually know her, did they?

People today are frightened by silence. There's a kind of inner loneliness. I think it's an agitated age. That's a comment, not a criticism.

It's a slow burner this coffin thing. Sorry about the pun.

> Some scientists predict that "in about five billion years", our sun will expand and evaporate the Earth, and thus end all life.

Frozen or not frozen?

Not frozen: Walt Disney (d.1966). American cartoon pioneer Disney is widely assumed to have been placed into cryogenic suspension. He was cremated and interred at Forest Lawn Memorial Park Cemetery.

Frozen: US baseball player Ted Williams (d.2002). Known as "the greatest hitter baseball has ever known", Williams's head is reported to have been removed and frozen in liquid nitrogen. His body is said to stand upright in a nine-foot tall cylindrical steel tank, also filled with liquid nitrogen. The procedure allegedly costs a cool $136,000.

Reincarnation
The rebirth in another body (after physical death) of some critical part of a person's personality or spirit. Its occurrence is a central tenet of Buddhism, Hinduism, Jainism, some African religions, as well as various other religions and philosophies.

Undead
The collective name for all types of corporeal and non-corporeal entities who were once alive in the normal sense, died, and then continued to exist in the world of the living. Examples include zombies (from the Voodoo religion), draugrs (from Norse mythology), vampires (various cultures) and hopping corpses (Chinese folklore).

> "A man who dares to waste one hour of time has not discovered the value of life."
>
> Charles Darwin (d.1882)

RIP Ian Dury (d.2000), **former lead singer with the Blockheads, has a memorial bench dedicated to him in Richmond Park, London, with *Reasons To Be Cheerful* carved in to it. It is solar-powered and enables people to plug into the bench and listen to Dury's music. Eight songs and an interview are available. (Note: requires own headphones.)**

Choosing a memorial
Almost anything can be carved out of wood or rock, so keep your options open. Options include a large pebble, the stump of a tree, an originally shaped gravestone, fences, stiles and benches.

Cost of a memorial bench

Hull City Council

Purchase of memorial wooden bench with memorial for a lease period of 10 years, where if available, a suitable site exists, and including installation of paving stones. (Fee does not include maintenance of bench.) Cost: £663.83 (plus £116 VAT).
Total: £780.
Renewal of ten-year lease: £250.
New memorial plate for bench: £100.
One-off refurbishment of memorial bench on request: £125.

Blackpool Council

£300 for the bench (includes delivery to site and installation).
Brass plaque: (if desired, will cost an additional £60).

Swindon Borough Council

Memorial bench seat: £670.
Memorial bench seat additional plaque: £136.

Weymouth & Portland Borough Council

Hardwood memorial bench, 5ft (including seat plaque) for a 10-year period: £600.
Additional 10-year period (only available after initial-lease period): £300.
Additional/replacement seat plaque: £29.

Joy Caplin is a Cruse bereavement counsellor

9/11 was a Tuesday. Our AGM was on the following Saturday and the Home Office asked for people who could drop everything and go to New York. We went the following Monday. It was surreal and bizarre. Everything was extraordinarily touching and New York was raw. The people were so nice; everyone was helpful. It was a life-changing event for me. I had that dusty taste in my mouth for six months. In fact, it's back right now. Every time I talk about it the taste comes back.

The absence of a body is always a lot more difficult to deal with. If a plane crashes, for example, it can be a help to visit the site. Seeing a body can be very helpful to the grieving process.

I specialise in bereavement through suicide. I facilitate a monthly group, all of whom have been bereaved through suicide. They come from miles around. Last month a man shouted at me and said I was useless, but you've got to be prepared for that. Anger and despair will be spat out at anyone nearby.

For older people, the death of a parent can often seem unbelievable. They think their parents are immortal.

I think the death of a child, an only child to a single mother, is the hardest to deal with, for me anyway. Everything is wrapped up in that child, the past, the future, future grandchildren. And then suddenly everything goes.

When women are bereaved, their status changes. They feel they are not wanted anymore, especially if their social life was as a couple. It's also true of men, but men often get people to look after them, offer to cook for them. There seems to be more care about for single men.

It's alright to have more than one feeling at the same time. You can love and hate at the same time. Over time, the grief remains the same, but people's lives continue to grow. So proportionally, the grief part becomes smaller.

I'm often embarrassed by my name. Joy is rather an inappropriate name for this job.

It is often thought that those who suffer the most are people who have had a long and steady relationship. But it's people who have had bad relationships that suffer more. There's suddenly no chance to mend the things that were wrong.

The problem, said my grandmother when she was 94, is not that her friends are dying, but rather that the friends of her daughter are dying.

It is estimated that each day 500 women become widows, while 175,000 men become widowers each year. Approximately 165,000 children under the age of 16 lose a parent each year, while about 12,000 children die in the UK each year.

What to do if bereaved?

- Talk to others about the loss, either family, friends, colleagues or experts.
- Bottling up grief, say experts, can cause future physical and mental problems.
- It takes most people one to two years to recover from a major bereavement.
- Tips: try to eat, sleep and exercise.
- GPs can prescribe sleeping pills, such as Loprazolam.
- Avoid making major decisions immediately following a bereavement.

Process of grieving

William J Worden (in his book Grief Counselling and Grief Therapy) says that mourning, which he defines as the emotional process that occurs after a loss, is an essential and painful healing process, which is achieved through a series of tasks:

1 Facing reality.
2 Experiencing the pain of grief.
3 Adjusting to the new reality.
4 Re-investing in the future and moving on with life.

Kids

Advice for children when it comes to grieving, as offered by the Child Bereavement Trust.

What is OK

- ✔ Cry and feel low and depressed.
- ✔ To feel angry, embarrassed and not want to talk about your feelings.
- ✔ Copy some of the activities and interests your brother or sister had before they died, but you need to retain your own life too.
- ✔ 'Live in the past' for a while. It can help you to keep alive the memory of your parent, your brother or sister, but try not to let life pass you by.
- ✔ Have fun and enjoy life, to laugh again and forget for a while, forgive yourself for the fights and arguments and nasty things you might have said to your parent, brother or sister who died.
- ✔ Go on living.

What's not OK

- ✗ Use drugs or excessive alcohol to dull your senses. This can only act as an escape and hide the pain, not helping to heal it, and it will then take longer to accept the hurt.

✘ Act out your frustration with reckless driving or skipping school.

✘ Do things with your anger that can hurt other people because you are hurting yourself.

✘ Experiment casually with sex, just to get close to someone.

✘ Hide your feelings and not talk about what is bothering you to protect your surviving parent.

✘ Act as the scapegoat or bad guy to appear tough.

Silence count

3-minute silence. For victims of Asian tsunami, suggested by the Luxembourg EU presidency in 2005.

2-minute silence. As a mark of respect for Queen Elizabeth the Queen Mother by all members, employees and offices of Buckingham County Council on 11 April 2002.

1-minute silence. To mark school hostage tragedy in Beslan, Russia (344 dead). For former Wigan Football Club manager Harry McNally. On the anniversary of the 11 September attack on the New York World Trade Centre (almost 3,000 dead). All British war dead (between one and two million dead).

Animal extinction (reasons for)
- Hunting/overharvesting.
- Introduction of alien species (such as rabbits, rats or cats).
- Habitat destruction.
- Pollution.

Some extinct animals
Dodo (est. 1681).
Great Auk (est. 1844, hunted for food and down for mattresses).
Cuban Shrew (est. 1910, introduction of predator).
Bali Tiger (last seen 1952).
Javan Tiger (1980s, overhunted).

Pet death

The death of a pet can lead to similar feelings as those experienced by people about other people dying. Natural reactions include anger, denial, grief and, finally, resolution.

What happens to pets?
According to the Association of Private Pet Cemeteries & Crematoria, one of the following courses of action is open after a pet death: individual burial or cremation; communal burial or cremation; communal cremation with separation of ashes; disposal by incineration; disposal by landfill; re-processing (bodies used for industrial or commercial purposes such as furs, fertiliser or animal feeds).

Dorothy Moore Brookes is chaplain at Great Ormond Street Hospital for Children

I met Jeremy on the first day of theological college, "the vicar factory" as we called it, in Cambridge.

The death of a child can be harrowing, but if they were born ill you can make sense of it. I can't make sense of a child hit by a bus.

I cry buckets at *EastEnders.* But when I cry I think I'm crying for all the Great Ormond Street children. Sometimes if I am baptising a dying child I cry.

Emotion at a funeral is appropriate. You laugh, you cry. After a funeral I potter around the garden. I need to be alone.

There's a lot of superstition around baptisms. We had a stillborn baby, who we called Matthew, and had him baptised. The church doesn't agree with it, but we believe every child is a gift. I think the experience has helped us deal with situations but there are still times when it feels as bad as it did at the very beginning. I still cry myself to sleep, but just not as often.

There is an aggressive element to suicide.

People always apologise for swearing in front of me.

I have bad hair days. It's hard to always be on duty, you have to be thoughtful. I mean, I can't shout at Jeremy in Sainsbury's car park.

Her husband Jeremy is a parish priest

People ask me what I do and it often stumps them. They make excuses about why they haven't been to church for so long. Not that I care!

I was the chaplain at Highgate Cemetery. The Victorians had an obsession with death.

I did three funerals in a day once. Each one was half the age of the one before. The last one was for a 23-year-old. It was massive and everyone turned up wearing Liverpool FC colours. I went to the do afterwards. The wake is very important for people.

It is significant for people to have me sit with them before they die. The dilemma is what prayer to say to a dying person. I sat with one old man who was dying for half an hour and didn't say a word. Finally, I turned to his wife and said let's say the Lord's Prayer. She said he smiled. He died 20 minutes later.

People don't know what comes after death. Sometimes it's grief and despair, sometimes grief and hope.

Sometimes it's good to speak ill of the dead. People laugh. If you go on about how they were a saint, when everyone knows they were not, you look like a fool.

Our neighbours ask us to bury their dead. We've done four funerals just in this close.

Live forever?

Being immortal means immunity to many aspects of mortality, fragile form, poor health and disease. The Immortality Institute is a US-based non-profit educational organisation whose mission is to "conquer the blight of involuntary death". It's based in Bethesda, Maryland.

RIP In 1843 William Miller (d.1849) **made the first of several predictions that the world would end in only a few months. None of them took place, but followers of Miller went on to found separate churches, the most successful of which is the Seventh-Day Adventist Church.**

RIP Born Michel de Nostredame in Saint-Rémy de Provence, in the south of France, Nostradamus (d.1566) **is one of Europe's most famous authors of prophecies. Jewish by birth, but raised a Roman Catholic, he studied medicine in Montpellier and was a pharmacist. His writings supposedly predicted the French Revolution, the assassination of Abraham Lincoln (d.1865), the Second World War and the rise to power of Adolf Hitler (d.1945).**

Heaven *n.* utopia, place of eternal happiness.

We're all universalists now

In Buddhism there are several heavens and those who accumulate good karma will be reborn in a heaven. However, their stay is not eternal – eventually they will use up all their good karma and be reincarnated as a human. Followers of universalism believe everyone will go to Heaven, no matter what they have done on earth.

Synonyms:

- afterworld
- Arcadia
- beyond
- bliss
- Canaan
- dreamland
- Elysium
- enchantment
- eternal home
- eternal rest
- eternity
- fairyland
- firmament
- great unknown
- harmony
- heights
- hereafter
- immortality
- kingdom
- kingdom come
- life everlasting
- next world
- nirvana
- paradise
- pearly gates
- promised land
- rapture
- Shangri-La
- sky
- the blue
- upstairs
- Utopia
- wonderland
- Zion

Believer?

Christianity tends to make entrance to Heaven conditional, not on good works but on having believed and trusted in the deity, and accepting the deity's offer of salvation. The phrase "Heaven and earth" is used to indicate the whole universe (Gen. 1:1; Jer. 23:24; Acts 17:24). The word "Heaven" originates from the Hebrew word "shamayim" meaning heights/elevations.

"My Jesus Mercy"

Epitaph, Al Capone (d.1947)

"To see a world in a grain of sand, And a Heaven in a wild flower, Hold infinity in the palm of your hand, And eternity in an hour"

William Blake (d.1827)

Religious martyrs (Christian)

Thomas a Becket (d.1170) Archbishop of Canterbury from 1162 to 1170, he was murdered in Canterbury Cathedral for opposing King Henry II.

Joan of Arc (d.1431) French heroine and military leader, inspired by religious visions to organise French resistance to the English and to have Charles VII crowned king. She was tried for heresy and burned at the stake.

Ten martyrs, whose statues stand above the western entrance to Westminster Abbey

1 **Maximilian Kolbe (d.1941)** Polish priest who offered to take the place of a condemned prisoner at Auschwitz. Patron of journalists, families, prisoners, the pro-life movement and the chemically addicted.
2 **Manche Masemola (d.1928)** Murdered by her parents for attending a Christian missionary school in Africa.
3 **Janani Luwum (d.1977)** Ugandan evangelist.
4 **St Elizabeth of Russia (d.1918)** Russian Orthodox philanthropist.
5 **Martin Luther King (d.1968)** American civil rights leader, he is considered one of the great prophetic leaders of the later twentieth century.
6 **Oscar Romero (d.1980)** A priest from El Salvador, he catalogued human rights abuses and was murdered while celebrating mass.
7 **Dietrich Bonhoeffer (d.1945)** German priest, murdered shortly before the end of the Second World War.
8 **Esther John (d.1960)** Pakistani Christian, she worked in orphanages and for women's rights until she was brutally murdered.
9 **Lucian Tapiedi (d.1942)** A Christian missionary born in Papua New Guinea.
10 **Wang Zhiming (d.1973)** A Chinese Christian.

Howard Greenoff runs Kingston cemetery

I have a reputation for being forthright but I don't give a shit.

You tend to fall into this industry by default. Either you have no education or you've been unemployed. I've worked on fairgrounds, been in the armed forces, been a pie-maker, a baker and a gravedigger. I did five years grave digging, by hand. It's hard work digging a nine-foot-deep hole.

Funeral directors have a lot of dedication. I did it once. It's a difficult job; a messy one. People might want to do everything for a loved one themselves but few understand what goes into it. The pillow under the head, the Vaseline on the eyelids, ensuring the nose and mouth are unblocked.

When I was part of the welly brigade [digging graves], people used to tell us we would never get anywhere. But you can in this business. Running a cemetery isn't hard. And don't let anyone tell you it is.

Death's still a taboo. People don't think about it. I mean, it's not as if you buy a coffin and stick it under your bed, inching it out for 25 years until you're ready to fall into it.

I find Rottweilers to be very intelligent dogs. And I tell you, they can hold a stare and work out people very quickly.

You get advice about sex and drugs at school, but never death. People aren't taught and they don't have a clue. There's all this fuss about pensions and saving for retirement, but what about the funeral? No one's telling people to save up for a funeral. I recommend people invest in a pre-arranged funeral.

I used to know a funeral director who'd cut the body's wrist with a razor. Just to make sure.

At one funeral, the hearse drew up but we couldn't open its back door. It was a screwdriver job. In the end, we had to get the family back into the other cars, drive them around the block and take the back window out.

Canon Morris used to do the fastest ever committals. So fast, he kept his bicycle clips on.

There's a lack of respect today. I was driving a hearse at a funeral once and had this bloke trying to overtake me! We get them all in the cemetery. Kids and grown adults, drinking, drunk. They don't care.

People shouldn't think they're being cheapskates when it comes to a funeral. I used to say to people, you can have that expensive coffin if you really want it, but we're only going to burn it.

I've seen fights at graveyards. Oh yeah. One group of blokes laying into another.

If I can push over a monument, it comes down. I'd rather that than some kid swings on it and it comes down on them. I call it "The Greenoff Shove".

We're a green lung. But cemeteries are black holes for cash.

Why do they use such old men as bearers? One funeral I was at, this old guy was backing towards the grave and fell in, dropping his end of the coffin. I've never seen so many people faint at one time, I swear. It could have got into *The Guinness Book of Records*.

Dr Eric Drexler, "the father of nanotechnology", and Massachusetts Institute of Technology's Dr Marvin Minsky, the founder of artificial intelligence (AI) research in the US, have been put into cryonic suspension. Dr James Bedford, a 73-year-old California psychology professor, was cryo-preserved on 12 January 1967.

700,000

Number of war memorials in the UK.

Death in the subtitles

- Flash Gordon Conquers the Universe (1940), aka "Purple Death from Outer Space."
- Indiana Jones and the Temple of Doom (1984), aka "Indiana Jones and the Temple of Death."
- The World Is Not Enough (1999), aka "Death Waits for No Man."
- Godfather: Part III, The (1990), aka "The Death of Michael Corleone."
- Tarzan's Magic Fountain (1949) aka "Tarzan and the Arrow of Death."

Don't panic!

Scientists are keen to predict The End Of The World As We Know It, taking over this mantle from the established church. The current favourite prediction for our impending doom is global warming, although Earth being hit by a massive asteroid remains a popular fear, and is backed up by a mass of frightening-looking statistics. Examples to beware of/be scared of include:

- A 50m asteroid hits our atmosphere roughly once a century, releasing the equivalent of 10 megatons of TNT in the explosion.
- A 1km asteroid hits the Earth every 100,000 years.
- Most tracking of known asteroids is done by amateur astronomers.
- There has been only one known victim of an object from outer space in the last century – a dog in Egypt in 1912.

Cremation

Cremation was practised in the ancient world, being mentioned in the *Old Testament* and used widely by the Greeks and Romans. It fell out of favour in the UK with an increased belief in the resurrection.

Cremation nation
Sir Henry Thompson, surgeon to Queen Victoria, was the first in the UK to recommend the practice on health grounds. In 1874 Thompson founded The Cremation Society of England. Woking Crematorium was founded in 1878 by Thompson. Famous people cremated there include Thomas Hardy, Dr Thomas Barnardo and the Marquis of Queensberry. In 1963 Pope John XXIII lifted the Roman Catholic ban on cremation and, in 1966, Pope Paul VI allowed Catholic priests to officiate at cremation ceremonies.

Religions that permit cremation
✔ Baptist church
✔ Buddhism
✔ Calvinism
✔ Christian Science
✔ Christian Churches of England, Scotland, Ireland and Wales
✔ Hare Krishna
✔ Hindu
✔ Jehovah's Witnesses
✔ Liberal Judaism
✔ Lutheranism
✔ Methodism
✔ Moravian Church
✔ Church of Jesus Christ of Latter-Day Saints (Mormons)
✔ Presbyterianism
✔ Roman Catholicism
✔ Salvation Army
✔ Seventh-Day Adventists
✔ Sikhs
✔ Society of Friends (Quakers)

Religions that forbid cremation
✘ Greek Orthodox Christianity
✘ Islam
✘ Orthodox Judaism
✘ Russian Orthodox Christianity
✘ Zoroastrianism

Cremation: for and against
Pros: cheap. No overcrowding issues.
Cons: pollution, especially mercury from fillings in teeth. Crematoriums are thought to be responsible for approximately 9% of airborne mercury emissions, caused by the combustion of dental amalgam; 12% of atmospheric dioxins, pollutants linked with cancer and other illnesses; and emissions of the chloride and formaldehyde used in the embalming process.

Jenny Gregson is a stonemason

Spelling mistakes do happen.
If you wanted a 15ft-high memorial you could ask the local council, but I know what they'd say. No.
The granite slabs come mostly from India and, increasingly, China. Most are already worked. It's all down to economics.
Most memorials all say the same thing.
Our advice to people is don't rush into it. People think they should sort out a headstone straight away, but everyone needs time to come to terms. They might change their minds after six months.
People usually start looking at gravestones two months after a death, but some come to see us before the funeral. Others might come to us two years after a death. And they still find it difficult.
There are a lot of health and safety rules and regulations today. In Bolton, all gravestones must be no taller than 3ft 6ins.
You never buy a grave, you buy a right of burial.
You don't really want to market this industry too much. People don't want to think that you're selling them a product. They want to think that you're helping them.
Most people when they come here don't want to be here. People often say to us: "Don't take this the wrong way but I hope I don't see you again." I understand that.
There was a Ukrainian buried near here and on his gravestone was etched, in Ukrainian, "here lies the man that killed my brother". Some of the Ukrainian community were in uproar and it had to be taken off. There are a lot of Ukrainians and Polish people around Rochdale.
Epitaphs are very regional, but people tend to use the same verses, to be honest. They avoid personal messages. I think people should go for more personal things myself.
People don't want to be different. It's a very English thing, I think. And they don't want to be seen to be skimping on the quality or cost. People worry a gravestone won't be high or thick enough.
The average cost for a typical black granite gravestone is £580, for this area. Some people take a deep intake of breath when they hear that, but others expect it to be at least £1,000. It depends. It would cost you more down south.
It takes at least two and sometimes three people to put up a gravestone.
There is a Christmas rush. It starts in October.

Colin Murray Parkes MD OBE is a consultant psychiatrist (St Christopher's and St Joseph's Hospices)

I have a Rwandan colleague. Her family had been wiped out in the genocide and the first thing she said to me when I met her was: "I'm dead." Now she's running a bereavement service in Rwanda that has given her life meaning and is helping others.

It's rare that I can't help someone, simply because of the experience I have.

The art of counselling is making people feel safe. A woman with cancer joined a discussion group of cancer patients. She came in and the first thing she said was that she hoped no one would talk about cancer. So everyone agreed. She talked about everything but cancer – her family, her doctor. Finally, when she felt safe, she started talking about cancer.

People try to find magical solutions when they are bereaved. A bereaved woman I knew married the best friend of her former husband just three months after her husband died.

It's tempting for doctors to talk down to people. After all, they have all this knowledge, this power. But it's a disastrous mistake. The most important thing is respect for patients.

I still intimidate people. I know that.

It's exciting when a client gets to the point when they start showing off about how well they are doing. One bereaved lady was enormously proud of the fact that she had been able to go out to the supermarket alone for the first time in months since the death of her husband. No one else would think twice about that, but I was full of admiration for her.

I dislike simple solutions to complex problems. I'd love to tell you how to solve the problems of the world but I cannot. I think respect and humility are important.

Who counsels the counsellor? My wife! You get used to it, but don't get hardened to it. I still care.

I hate disasters, but I keep getting involved in them. My first was Aberfan in 1966. It was very traumatic; I was helpless. Now I realise that, although you can make a difference, there is a limit to what any one person can achieve.

I'm not normally aware that I bottle things up, but I know I am sometimes because I dream about things.

People ask me if I'm prepared for my own death. I've had moments when I've been ill and thought about it, but I'm often more concerned for my family.

I'm more concerned by dying than by death. There are painful deaths. I hope mine is a quiet one.

In my teens I was an ardent atheist. But after working in hospices I come into contact with strong religious beliefs and I am less judgemental. I don't have an easy answer but I respect that there are different ways of thinking.

Dame Cicely Saunders (d.2005): **The world's first ever hospice, St Christopher's Hospice, Sydenham, south London, was founded by Cicely Saunders in 1967. Before this date, terminally ill patients were rarely treated with appropriate painkillers (morphine was considered addictive and too dangerous to administer to terminally ill people).**

2,500

Cyclists killed or seriously injured each year in the UK. About one-quarter of the cyclists killed are children. Four out of five cyclist casualties are male.

4,000

Deaths each year as a result of accidents at home. About 350 of these are under 25 years old and 1,500 aged over 75. Of the 120 children under 14 that die at home each year, 27 die from poisoning.

"To me, old age is always 15 years older than I am"

US statesman Bernard Mannes Baruch (1870-1965), quoted in *Newsweek* on his 85th birthday.

Time to die?

Start worrying at ages 50-54. In 1989, 15,053 people between that age died. Between 55 and 60 years old, about a third to a half more men die than women. From 61 to 64, between 6,000 and 10,000 more men than women die each year. Then it's just one-way traffic. At least an extra 10,000 more men than women die aged 65-69 and so the pattern continues. More and more people are making it to 95 and over, with a record 21,877 people passing that age in 2001. It's more than five times likely to be a woman.

Suicidal?

Young females in the 15-24 age group are at the lowest risk. The suicide rate for this group has remained fairly constant since 1979 and is now about three per 100,000 population. Women born in India and East Africa have a 40% higher suicide rate than those born in England and Wales. The suicide rate among young Asian women is twice that of the national average, according to the charity MIND.

Charles Stewart Rolls (d. 1910) **Buried at St Cadoc's Church, Llangattock-Vibon-Avel, Monmouthshire. A speed freak and friend of car maker F.H. Royce, Rolls was one of the first auto enthusiasts to break the**

4mph speed limit in 1896. A fan of ballooning, in 1910 he received certificate number two from the Royal Aero Club to fly planes. He became the first man to fly non-stop across the English Channel both ways. He died in 1910 when the French-built Wright biplane he was flying in broke up. He was Britain's first aircraft fatality.

Captain L.E.G. Oates (d.1912) died "outside", in Antarctica. Oates, a cavalry officer and Boer War hero, committed suicide on his 32nd birthday by walking out into a blizzard during Robert Falcon Scott's fateful last expedition. Scott also died in Antarctica, along with Chief Petty Officer Edgar "Taff" Evans, surgeon Dr Edward Wilson and Lieutenant Henry Bowers.

Great things to have named after you

- **Comet.** A graduate of Oxford and a member of The Royal Society at the age of 22, Edmond Halley (d.1742) is best remembered for the comet that he first predicted to return.

- **Crater.** Charles Babbage (d.1871) is buried at Kensal Green Cemetery (his brain is preserved in Lincoln's Inn, London). Considered the "father of computing", Babbage was ridiculed while alive. He now has a moon crater named after him.

- **Country.** Simon Bolivar (d.1830) was one of South America's greatest generals. His victories over the Spanish won independence for Bolivia, Panama, Colombia, Ecuador, Peru and Venezuela. He is called El Libertador (The Liberator) and the "George Washington of South America". He became dictator of Peru and, in 1825, Upper Peru became a separate state, called Bolivia.

- **Regions/places.** Abel Janszoon Tasman (d.1659) was born in the village of Lutjegast, in the Netherlands, in 1603. In 1633 Tasman signed up with the Dutch East India Company. Looking for the famed Southern Continent, in November 1642, he sighted the west coast of Tasmania, which he named Van Diemen's Land. In 1855 the island's name was changed to Tasmania.

- **Body part.** Achilles. One of the greatest of the Greek warriors at Troy, he was invulnerable except for his heel (which his mother the sea-nymph Thetis had held as she dipped her baby into the River Styx). He was eventually killed, shot in the heel, by Priam's son Paris.

"In heaven, all the interesting people are missing."
Friedrich Wilhelm Nietzsche (d.1900)

Alan Gale MM is a Chelsea Pensioner

I was born in Lambeth Workhouse in 1919, but my mother died when I was four and I was put into care. That's a funny name for it though.

I had a bully for a father, who hit and beat me. Once, when I came home from work aged 18, he laid into me again. This time I laid into him. The very next day I left and joined the army. That was 1936.

One of my first roles in the army was reconnaissance. We crossed over the French line of defence into German territory to collect mines. Then we'd take them back and see how they worked.

I know I've got a brother and sister somewhere but I only ever met them when I was small.

If you're facing a Panzer unit, you're scared. But you can fight them and we did. We had ingenuity and we taught them a thing or two.

We were surrounded by death.

I believe in God. I'm an ardent believer. If I'm ever in trouble I talk to God and I know He has been there for me. Because I believe in God I can face death. If He wants me, I'll go to Him.

When we got to Dunkirk I didn't think we'd make it. I prayed and asked God to allow me to do my duty to Him and to my country. An hour later we blew up the harbour wall and we made it onto a boat and then onto a destroyer and home.

You never volunteer. That's the rule.

I was awarded the Military Medal for service in North Africa, while I was in charge of a patrol. Our mission was to clear a minefield for an attack that was to follow. I disarmed 40 telemines, all booby-trapped, and I got up to within a few metres of the enemy lines without them seeing me. They were asleep!

When you are fighting it occurs to you that you could die. You know you could be shot any time. But it never tested my faith in God. I got shot in the finger, in the leg, and I've got a curvature of the spine from a blow to the back of the neck from a German during hand-to-hand fighting. They didn't just let us walk into their trenches, you know.

I had a lousy wife. She became a Jehovah's Witness.

You have to forgive and forget, but you must be aware that countries could rise up and do the same again if left unchecked. I don't think Germany will now because of the EU. And of course the nuclear bomb is the big deterrent.

The worst thing about getting older is that you're not as fit as you used to be. But before I had a stroke and lost some memory I felt as young as I ever had.

If I ever win the Lottery, I'll give most of it to help the starving Africans.

If someone doesn't believe in God, they will fight to the last breath. After all, it's all they've got.

Hell is...

A place of torment, of great weeping and gnashing of teeth. The word "Hell" is derived from the Old English "Hel", meaning underworld, as well as the name of the goddess of the underworld. In most religions' concept of Hell, "evildoers" will suffer eternally in Hell after their death.

The Bible refers to Hell as "Gehenna", from the valley of Gai-Hinnom, a valley near Jerusalem where, in ancient times, garbage was burned. Some scholars believe the association of fire with hell comes from volcanic eruptions.

The Rabbinic Jewish view of Hell: the longest that one can be there is said to be 12 months. Christians says Hell is a place ruled by the Devil, or Satan (the former angel cast out from Heaven).

Rub it in
According to Luke (Chapter 16:19-28) nobody can pass from Hell to Heaven or vice versa. Fire is not the only torment. Thirst is another. To rub it in, those who are in Hell are said to be able to see the happiness reigning in Heaven, and those in Heaven do not feel compassion for the others in Hell.

Hold that thought
Salisbury Cathedral was completed by 1258, with its spire, the tallest in England (404ft), added later. A 13th century doorway shows the faithful ascending to Heaven while hairy devils drag the damned into the mouth of Hell.

People whose first names start with the letter J with airports named after them
- US president John F Kennedy (d.1963).
- Jose Maria Cordova (d.1846), a Peruvian soldier.
- John Lennon, former Beatle (d.1980).
- Pope John Paul II (d.2005).
- Actor John Wayne (d.1979).

Dante Alighieri (d.1321): **Italian poet and author of *The Divine Comedy*, describes an image of Hell with the inscription at its entrance: "Abandon all hope, you who enter here." A similar message is displayed on some road signs pointing towards the M25.**

Norwich and the paupers
During the 18th century, churchyards became crowded, particularly in the cities. The poor had to settle for pauper graves, where up to 20 bodies shared a single grave, which was kept open until it was full, each body only covered lightly with earth. It was the resulting public-health hazards that led to the first non-church related burial sites, otherwise known as cemeteries. The first English cemetery, the Rosary, was opened in Norwich in 1819.

Not so great things to have named after you: Diseases. Parkinson's disease is named after Dr James Parkinson (d.1824).

Lifetime odds of how US citizens will die

Cause of death	Lifetime odds
Motor vehicle accidents	82:1
Assault by firearm	315:1
Motorcycle riding	1,159:1
Exposure to smoke, fire and flames	1,179:1
Fall on and from stairs and steps	2,331:1
Cycling	4,857:1
Firearms discharge	4,888:1
Air and space transport accidents	5,704:1
Contact with machinery	5,713:1
Drowning and submersion while in or falling into swimming-pool	5,857:1
Lightning	56,439:1
Cataclysmic storm	59,127:1
Earthquake and other earth movements	120,161:1
Railway or railway vehicle accidents	133,035:1
Bitten or struck by dog	206,944:1
Fireworks discharge	744,997:1

Source: Insurance Information Institute

Living memorial

The National Memorial Arboretum is located between Lichfield and Burton on Trent, just off the A38 on the A513 signposted for Tamworth. Since March 1997 more than 60,000 trees have been planted on the site and over 100 dedicated plots created. The idea for it, a living reminder of the 80 million lives lost in the conflicts of the twentieth and twenty-first centuries, was conceived by David Childs, the founding director, after a visit to Arlington Cemetery in Washington. The site features the statue of a blindfolded 17-year-old Northumberland Fusilier executed by firing squad at Ypres in 1915.

What do different grave symbols mean?

Cross = symbolises the mode of death of Jesus Christ.
Broken column = signifies a life cut short.
Anchor = early Christian symbol of hope.
Coiled snake = eternity.
Two hands clasped together = means farewell, with broken chain underneath representing the death of a family member.
Heart pierced by a sword = symbolises the Virgin Mary.
Rock = symbolises Christ.

Unlucky?

The most widely held superstitious belief in the UK is touching wood, which 86% said they did, according to Professor Richard Wiseman, chair of Public Understanding of Psychology at the University of Hertfordshire. Sixty-four per cent of people said they cross their fingers, while 49% avoid walking under ladders. This superstition is said to stem from the days of capital punishment. When being hanged, the condemned person would be made to pass underneath a ladder before climbing it and onto the gallows.

Dave Bingham is chairman of the
British Psychic & Astrological Society

I was in the medical corps in the army in 1958. I think that was the start of my understanding of my psychic self. You get a lot of free time in the army. You sleep, you relax, you get very relaxed. The next thing you know, you're on the ceiling, looking down at yourself. The first time it happened I panicked, but then I spoke about it with my sergeant who was a Zen Buddhist. He told me what was happening and that astral travel was possible.

I read sand. You find out a lot about people's emotions with sand reading. I'm not an astrologer per se, I'm more intuitive. I've always been close to nature.

Our society is there as a certification organisation. The same way Corgi does gas.

I have handed out cautions to people who come for a reading; told people to avoid situations in which they could lose their life. It's a bad reader who tells someone they are about to die.

Technically I'm Pagan now. I try not to carry the clutter of Christianity. I can't believe in Heaven and Hell or the Devil. Clerics put Heaven and Hell there for control. I believe there's a universal force, and that we are part of it.

Some clairvoyants see pictures, some hear things, some feel pain, smell or taste things. Being a medium is about making contact with the energies of those that have gone before. You pick up whatever they want to throw at you. I've seen a table tipping during a seance in Brighton.

Tony Blair's got funny hands. He's got a Simian Line, that's a concentration of the head and heart line. That means he is very intense, very focused. It's unusual.

With the occult, you need to know how to close doors as well as open them.

What's a ghost? It's energy. It's people not knowing they are dead. I had a friend who was having a problem in his flat. It was cold in one room and he asked if I could have a look. The room had a three-bar electric heater in it on full blast, but the room was like a fridge. So I tapped in to the energy and I picked up a feeling of a chap who had had a car accident. He was waiting for somebody. His girlfriend had also been in the car but she was in hospital in intensive care. The man wanted to know if she was coming too, but she wasn't. She was going to live, that was the answer. Suddenly, the room temperature went so high we had to open the window.

I thought that with you writing a book about death you'd be a Scorpio. They either love or fear death.

We've got a vicar as a member. He does house clearances for us.

Elvis had a morbid fascination with death. He used to take his girlfriends to the mortuary.

What is normal?

"Practically immortal"

The Red Sea urchin, found in the Pacific Ocean, is one of Earth's longest-living animals. It can live for more than 200 years. "No animal lives forever, but these Red Sea urchins appear to be practically immortal," says marine zoologist at Ohio State University, Dr Thomas Ebert.

Party like it's 12006

A perfectly frozen person is expected to remain "physically viable" for a period of about 10,000 years.

120

Number of people being cryonically preserved, as of 2004. All are in the US.

0

Number of cryopreserved humans or other mammals that have been revived.

Possible problems with cryogenics

Power cuts.
Grogginess.
Out-of-date wardrobe.
Waking up and finding that nothing had changed.
Waking up and finding that everyone else has died.

Cryogenic patients are stored upside down.

Where to go in the US

1 Alcor Life Extension Foundation, Scottsdale, Arizona: www.alcor.org
2 The American Cryonics Society, Cupertino, California: www.americancryonics.org
3 Cryonics Institute, Clinton Township, Michigan: www.cryonics.org
4 Trans Time, California: www.transtime.com

On 16 March 2880, there is a one-in-300 probability that asteroid 1950DA will hit Earth, causing "an extinction-level event".

First and Second World Wars

887,282

UK personnel killed in the First World War.

382,677

UK personnel killed in the Second World War. For every 10 UK persons killed in the 1939–45 war, 23 were killed in the 1914–18 war.

Ghostly places

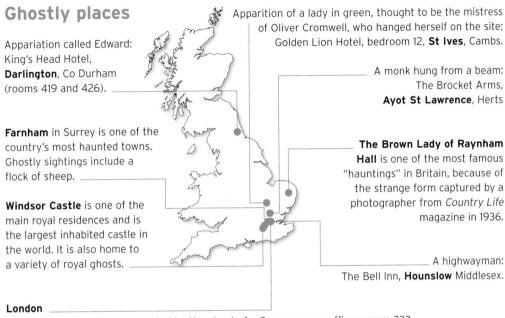

Appariation called Edward: King's Head Hotel, **Darlington**, Co Durham (rooms 419 and 426).

Apparition of a lady in green, thought to be the mistress of Oliver Cromwell, who hanged herself on the site: Golden Lion Hotel, bedroom 12, **St Ives**, Cambs.

A monk hung from a beam: The Brocket Arms, **Ayot St Lawrence**, Herts

Farnham in Surrey is one of the country's most haunted towns. Ghostly sightings include a flock of sheep.

Windsor Castle is one of the main royal residences and is the largest inhabited castle in the world. It is also home to a variety of royal ghosts.

The Brown Lady of Raynham Hall is one of the most famous "hauntings" in Britain, because of the strange form captured by a photographer from *Country Life* magazine in 1936.

A highwayman: The Bell Inn, **Hounslow** Middlesex.

London
- The Langham Hotel, is haunted by the ghost of a German army officer: room 333.
- Chanting monks from the Middle Ages: St Dunstan's Church, East Acton.
- The Grey Lady. Top left-hand box, facing the stage, Theatre Royal, Drury Lane, London.
- The Grenadier pub, Belgravia. Army officer caught cheating at cards. He was whipped to death in the cellar.

Ghost *n.* a disembodied spirit, a ghost is supposedly a soul that cannot find rest after death. Often seen as "unfinished business", such as a victim seeking justice or revenge after death, or a criminal lingering to avoid Hell.

"It's funny how most people love the dead, once you're dead you're made for life." Jimi Hendrix (d.1970)

"Learn as if you were going to live forever. Live as if you were going to die tomorrow." Mahatma Gandhi (d.1948)

"Fear not death, for the sooner we die the longer we shall be immortal." Benjamin Franklin (d.1790)

"I have never killed a man, but I have read many obituaries with great pleasure." Clarence Darrow (d.1938)

"To himself everyone is immortal; he may know that he is going to die, but he can never know that he is dead." Samuel Butler (d.1902)

"Life does not cease to be funny when people die any more than it ceases to be serious when people laugh." George Bernard Shaw (d.1950)

"Either he's dead or my watch has stopped." Groucho Marx (d.1977)

"Death may be the greatest of all human blessings." Socrates (d.399BC)

DEAD INFO

SOURCES

Dead serious

Cruse Bereavement Care, Office for National Statistics (ONS), Prison Reform Trust, *Bible*, Westminster Abbey, BBC, Royal Society for the Prevention of Accidents (RoSPA), National Association for Mental Health (MIND), British Heart Foundation, University of Oxford Centre for Suicide Research, The UK Guild of Taxidermists, *London Blue Plaque Guide*, Voluntary Euthanasia Society, NOP.

Dead calm

National Health Service, Association of Anatomical Pathology Technologists, *The Natural Death Handbook*, *Bhagavad Gita*, *Holy Qur'an*, *The English Way of Death* by Julian Litten, *Tibetan Book of Living & Dying*, Home Office, ONS, Flowers & Plants Association, Interflora, Depression Alliance.

Dead & buried

The Natural Death Handbook, The Cremation Society of Great Britain, BBC, LifeGem, Mintel, *Survey Of Funeral Costs In Britain 2000*, commissioned by The Oddfellows, Department for Environment, Food and Rural Affairs, *British Journal of Psychiatry*.

Dead ahead

Human Genome Project, Department of Health (UK), Inland Revenue, Cancer Research, Cruse Bereavement Care, RoSPA, ONS, *Bible*.

With thanks to:

Vicky, for everything. Also, thanks to Cristian Barnett for his enthusiasm, fantastic eye for a picture and limitless energy without whom there would be no book. Jenny Eade for her strict deadline setting and design excellence. And thank you to Craig Saxon for his input, random knowledge and general cynicism. Many thanks to Paul, Clare, Heather and Clare at The Friday Project for being lovely and making this book a reality. All power to you. Each and every one of the interviewees who were charming, generous and open and who between them gave me lifts, cups of tea, somewhere to stay, extremely useful advice, lunch, jokes, secrets, warnings and insights. Particular mentions to Roslyn Cassidy, a remarkable lady with impeccable contacts. To Paul Sinclair, a good man on a mission. To Carl Marlow, for hospitality, honesty and Geordie charm. Also deserving of praise: Hannah for her excellent contacts. Brian Parsons, great house, great stuffed animals. Kate at ifishoulddie. Thanks to Hazel at ecopods in Brighton. Bob and Sheri Coates, both lovely people (Sheri, surely the most glamorous lady in the world of death). Annie Kiff-Wood, Alan and Colin at Cruse Bereavement Care. Professor Julian Litten. The nice people at The Natural Death Centre in London, especially Michael Jarvis. Author and enthusiast John Clarke. Alison Holding at the Office for National Statistics. The good people at Caspian Publishing for all manner of help and support, particularly Andrea St. Hill, Francesca Cunningham, Matthew Rock, Erroll Jones and Ric Wadsworth. And special thanks to Gary Pickett. Cheers to Sharon Robinson for her help and contribution. Final thanks to Brian Henderson at swebtec, Rachel James and Leigh Nissim. Also Toby Allen, Kate Murphy, Oli Barrett, Becky Senior, Meric Pine, Fizz, Duncan Cheatle, Baroness Greengross and the incomparable Keith Elliott. Finally, thanks to my lovely family.

Cristian: thanks very much to Jackie for her patience, encouragement and willingness to visit graveyards on wet Sundays. Jenny: thanks to Jamie for asking me to design his book. And a huge thanks to my lovely Knoll - for everything.

GENERAL & PRACTICAL HELP

Advice for the living

Try and keep all your affairs in order, at least keeping the paperwork in one place so that if you do die (because you are going to) those left behind aren't faced with an impossible and harrowing task. Also, any plans you do make regarding your own demise, make sure you tell someone or write it down and tell them where it is. The last thing the family will want, after watching the coffin go through to the incinerator, is to come across a note from you stating your desire to be buried at sea. It does happen.

Good to talk

- Talk about a bereavement to family, friends or professionals.
- Tell your doctor.
- Homeopaths can be helpful.
- Talk to professional organisations (such as Cruse, see list).

Newspaper obituaries

When placing a death notice in the papers, be ready for a response. Have a friend or relation on hand to field calls that might come in from long-lost friends or work colleagues. Otherwise you may find yourself endlessly repeating the story of the final days and hours and this can be traumatic. It means you're not having to deal with other people's hysterics plus you're not on

the phone a lot and don't become fearful of answering it.

How to grieve

Rule one: there are no rules. Bereaved people go through emotions ranging from guilt to anger, sadness to relief, sometimes feeling more than one emotion at the same time. It's natural. Don't turn to drink or drugs as this only postpones the grieving. Try and speak to people about how you feel. Although the feeling or loss will remain, simply continuing to live means that, proportionally, it will start to represent a smaller part of you. Hence the cliché, "time is the best healer". Avoid "throwing yourself into your work" or trying to act like nothing has happened. It has happened and the quicker you deal with it the better for you, your health and your relationships. It's not unusual to have dreams or thoughts about the deceased. Men − it's good to cry. Also, talk to the kids. They know something has happened. Be straight with them.

Documents

It is important to check thoroughly any documents you may be sent following the death of someone close to you. Get a neighbour, friends or relative to double-check letters you send or receive. Mistakes easily happen and processes take much longer. You can't get enough death certificates. Everyone you contact, from social services to the local library, wants one and maybe needs one. Some organisations will accept photocopies but not all. Get them all at one time, it saves hassle.

How to choose a funeral director (and how to deal with them)

- Shop around. Get a friend to do it if it's too distressing. In fact, although organising a funeral yourself can be a cathartic experience, having a less emotional friend along to help make the important decisions makes a big difference.
- Anyone can be a funeral director and belonging to one of the two main trade bodies, although preferable, doesn't guarantee service. The main two are the National Association of Funeral Directors (NAFD) and The National Society of Allied and Independent Funeral Directors (SAIF). Any complaints, speak to Citizens Advice.
- Don't think that getting the best price implies you are a cheapskate or that it somehow makes you a bad person, or that you did not love the deceased person. Haggle! Why not? Most funeral directors need the work so they will do you a deal if you are persistent.
- If you want a particular type of coffin, but not one in the funeral director's glossy brochure, why not get it yourself from elsewhere? After all, it's either going up in smoke or down into the ground. Many firms make affordable coffins and you can always decorate it.

Alternatively, any carpenter should be able to knock one up. The funeral director might not like it, but that's only because of the healthy mark-ups on coffins.

- Get the quote in writing, and in full. Check there are no hidden extras.
- There are no rules when it comes to a funeral and you can, so long as it is within the law, do what you want. Don't feel pressured into using hearses if you don't need or want them. Take a cab, save some money for the wake afterwards or for buying something to cheer you up.
- If you want to organise flowers yourself, do it. Some funeral directors will have deals with florists and will encourage you to use the company they suggest.
- If you want to have the body at home for a day or two, that's not a problem and the funeral director should help you.
- A good funeral director should be a facilitator, meaning they should be there to help you do what you want. If you sense that they are trying to saddle you with unnecessary items or costs, tell them and refuse the items.

Who to inform when someone dies?

Many will require death certificates. Boring and upsetting, but it must be done. Here is a list of most of them.

Vehicle registration (DVLA)
Passport office
Motoring insurance
Motor breakdown policy
Household insurance
Life assurance

Pension provider
Bank or building society
Credit card companies
Utilities (gas, electricity, water, telephone)
Council Tax
Benefit agency
Inland Revenue
Mortgage provider
Internet provider
Child(ren)'s school or childcare provider
Doctors, dentists, hospital clinics
Private health care provider
Solicitor
Season tickets
Library
National insurance.

Note: if the deceased owned a vehicle then it may be no one now has insurance cover to drive it. Many policies state that a vehicle may be driven by someone else with the owner's permission, but as soon as the owner dies any such permission may cease. Contact the car insurance company before anyone drives the vehicle to make sure they are covered.

Pre-paid funerals

If you are arranging a funeral, try to find out if the deceased had made any arrangements. If you are buying a pre-paid funeral plan for yourself read the contract carefully. The contract terms must be fair and not put you at a disadvantage in relation to the plan provider. If you are in doubt about any terms get advice from the local Citizens Advice Bureau. Also see your local trading standards department

(www.tradingstandards.gov.uk, or you can find its details in the phone book under the local authority). In Northern Ireland contact the trading standards branch of the Department of Enterprise, Trade and Investment.

Check what the contract covers and what it doesn't. Find out what should happen after you die and leave appropriate instructions with your solicitor or next of kin, as an incorrect decision could cause problems. Shop around and check whether a plan provider is a member of one of the trade associations who are members of the Funeral Ombudsman Scheme.

Questions to ask providers of pre-paid funerals

- What happens if you die before payments are completed?
- What happens if you chose a funeral director who goes out of business?
- How is your money protected over the years?
- What happens to the money you have paid if relatives do not know of the pre-paid plan and organise the funeral independently?

Home contents and insurance

Any home or contents insurance policy may become void once one of the owners dies. If a single person dies, the cover may also stop if there is no one living in the house full time. It is advisable to check with the policy provider.

Selling the house of a deceased relative

Don't simply leave the property unattended. If it's difficult, take a competent relative or friend.

Ensure heating, water and electrics remain in good working order. When it comes to selling the property, these things are important.

Possessions

Another tricky one and something you may be better facing with a relative or friend. First of all, try and ensure that all interested parties agree – often easier said than done. The most important aspect of disposing of a deceased relative's belongings (especially those not covered in a Will) is not to be rash. Leave it a month if it's too traumatic. Don't stick it all on a bonfire the next day. Better still, give it to charity. Do some good.

Picking music for funerals in crematoria
Do:
- ✓ choose whatever music you wish (bear in mind the poor-quality stereo systems in crematoria).
- ✓ take the correct CD.
- ✓ ensure whoever is in charge of the music knows what song you want played and at what point.
- ✓ bear in mind the length of time you have in the crematorium (that is, avoid ten-minute long orchestral recitals if you only have half an hour and eight people are due to speak).

Don't:
- ✗ play the wrong music. If the bereaved liked Megadeth, play Megadeth. If they enjoyed the BBC's Shipping Forecast, play that. There are no rules (unless at a Humanist ceremony, where religious music is not permitted).
- ✗ rely on the music being at the crematorium.
- ✗ get carried away and think you can sing an operatic solo in the crematorium (unless you really can).

DEATH, THE LAW AND YOU

The legal implications of a death are complicated. Horrendously so. What with the funeral to arrange, mourning to do, plus house and contents to sort out, the last thing anyone needs is to grapple with the intricacies and brutal reality of the British legal system. Of the many pitfalls, not having a Will is probably the most common. Who wants to think about it? At least half the population don't. But it definitely adds to the problems of those left behind, so the advice is: sort it out. It's cheap to make a Will and shouldn't take long. It is advisable to employ a solicitor at the outset, to ensure that wishes are met and inheritance tax liability minimised. The average cost of going to a solicitor is about £65 for a single Will or £95 for a couple. Additional advice on inheritance tax may bring the cost closer to £200.

Legal glossary

Beneficiaries: Those who inherit your estate when you die. There is no limit to the number of beneficiaries.

Codicil: An addition or amendment to your Will.

Chattels: Any moveable possessions.

Deed: A written, signed legal document that sets out things to be done. Most often used in the context of property, where transactions are in writing and signed.

Discretionary trust: A trust where the trustee has full power to decide which members of a group of beneficiaries are to receive their income or capital and when.

Estate: The property, money and possessions of the deceased person.

Executor: Person appointed to administer your Will when you die.

Guardians: the people chosen by the testator to look after their children in the event of their death.

Inheritance Tax: This is a tax that is levied against your estate at the time of your death.

Intestate: To die without making a legally valid Will.

Living Will: A Living Will or "advance directive" is a document containing instructions issued to medical personnel to allow them to stop prolonging your life in the event of you becoming terminally ill, permanently unconscious or losing your mental capacity. Some people decide they do not want to be kept alive in such an event by either artificial means or medical treatment. Legally, Living Wills cannot necessarily be enforced by law.

Pecuniary legacies: Pecuniary legacies are set amounts of money to be left to specific people.

Probate: When somebody dies the person dealing with the Will has to obtain probate from their local Probate Registry as evidence of the validity of the Will that they will administer.

Residue: What's left after pecuniary legacies, specific gifts, funeral, inheritance tax, including bank accounts and insurance policies.

Revocation: If the testator decides to change their Will completely and it invalidates the previous one they are deemed to have "revoked" the previous Will.

Specific gifts: Specific gifts are gifts you want left to specific people, such as leaving your pet cat to a specific individual you know would be happy to look after it.

Testator: The person who actually sets out his or her wishes and requests as to how their estate should be divided in the form of a Will. A Testator must be over 18 years of age and of sound mind at the time of writing the Will.

Trustees: The trustees hold on to any assets set out in the Will until the nominated beneficiaries meet certain criteria set out in the Will, for example they reach the age of 18. Trustees normally have powers to distribute monies and have full power to sell and invest. When you die, the executors are the trustees of your property that they give to your beneficiaries. If children inherit property it must be held in trust until they reach the age of 18. You may appoint your executors or anyone else you choose as your trustees.

Witnesses: A Will is always subject to two witnesses who will have to verify the signature of the testator. They will have to sign the Will at the same time as each other and also at the same time as the testator.

Dying without a Will (or dying intestate)

Your family will be left to sort out the administrative details of your death. They will not be able to decide what happens to your estate as it will be administered in accordance with strict rules and regulations known as "Rules of Intestacy". A legal professional may have to be enlisted to assist them with this. Neither yourself or your family will have any control over what happens to your estate and it will not automatically be divided between members of your family. You will not be able to make sure that particular gifts are left to the right friends, family and charities.

If married but no Will

If you are married and do not have a Will the amount your spouse can inherit is limited by the Government.

1 If the estate is worth less than £125,000 your spouse will receive everything.
2 If it is worth more, and there are no children or relatives, your spouse will receive everything and inheritance tax will be payable on everything over £242,000.
3 If there are children then your spouse will receive £125,000 plus personal chattels and the rest of the estate is divided into two. The children receive one half and the other half is held on trust. The spouse then receives income arising from that trust over his or her lifetime.
4 If there are no children, then the spouse is entitled to the first £200,000, plus personal chattels and the rest of the estate is divided into two. The parents (or brothers and sisters) receive one half and the other half is held on trust. The spouse then receives income arising from that trust over his or her lifetime.
5 If there is no spouse and no living relatives then the estate will automatically go to the Crown.

If cohabiting

When you live with a partner for a few years, they become your common-law husband or wife. Common-law wives and husbands do not have the same rights as married persons and if you do not have a Will then your estate will be divided up as if you were a single person.

If single

If you are single and die intestate, then there is a chain of people who will inherit. In the first instance everything will go to your children. If you have no children, then it will be your grandchildren. If you have no grandchildren, then it will go to both your parents. If your parents are no longer alive, then it will go to your brothers and sisters. And if you have no brothers and sisters, then it will go to your nieces and nephews. If you have no nieces and nephews then it will go to your grandparents, then aunts and uncles and lastly cousins. If you have no family members whatsoever then your estate will go to the Government.

Executor

If you have agreed to become an executor or are considering becoming one, it is important to understand exactly what is involved. An executor sorts out the administrative details of a Will as detailed below. Executors have usually been specifically named to act in a Will. If a person has not been named but wants to become an executor they can apply for an administrative grant to the Probate Registry. An executor's role is for life because new additions or claims to the estate can arise in the future. An executor can, of course, decline to act but this would have to be confirmed to the Probate Registry in writing. There can be a maximum of four executors named in any one Will, but the standard is usually two.

Administration

An executor has to carry out certain tasks in order to legally fulfil the obligations of the task. An executor should therefore:

1 Notify family, friends and workplace colleagues of the death. This can include placing details in the local/national paper along with funeral details so that people can attend if they wish.

2 Obtain a copy of the medical certificate indicating the cause of death and a formal notice from the doctor.

3 Register the death at the local Registry of Births, Deaths and Marriages. The death must be registered in order to obtain the death certificate. The registrar will also issue a disposal certificate to allow you to dispose of the body in the chosen way.

4 Make sure they have the last original Will of the deceased. The testator should have already informed the executors where the Will is kept.

5 Make copies for beneficiaries, banks, Inland Revenue, for example, then put the Will away. It is important that the original Will is not tampered with in anyway (including the addition of staples etc).

6 Pay any inheritance tax if necessary.

7 Contact the local Probate Registry to obtain either your grant of probate (if there is a Will and you are named as executor) or your grant of administration (if there is no Will but you seek to become the executor).

8 Draw up simple accounts providing details of how the estate has been divided. An income tax form will also need to be completed for the deceased. Note: It is advisable to open a separate account into which money paid into the estate can be credited. This will prevent estate money becoming confused with personal finances.

9 Deal with the funeral arrangements or assist whomever is dealing with them to ensure that the wishes of the deceased are carried out as far as possible. Note: It is not always possible to follow the wishes of the deceased if conflicts arise. For example, if the deceased requested

that their body should be available for transplant or for medical science, the executor would still need the permission of the next of kin before this could go ahead. The next of kin have the legal right to deny consent.

10 Notify all businesses of the death, for example, utilities, credit card companies, banks, building societies, council tax office, social security and tax office. It is also worth giving the post office a change-of-address form so that any post will be redirected straight to you.

11 Gather all documents relevant to the Will and compile a list of assets, debts and liabilities. Debts and liabilities should be paid off and funeral expenses should be taken from the amount. The remainder can then be distributed accordingly.

12 Distribute the contents of the Will, making sure that if anything is left to children under the age of 18, a trustee has been named. This will include the distribution of pecuniary, specific gifts and legacies where applicable and the distribution of the residue. See legal terms for more information.

If not you, then who?

If you appoint one of the big banks as executor you or your family will have to pay about £10,000 for an estate valued at £250,000, whereas solicitors typically charge £5,000 for an average estate (see Table 1).

What is probate?

Probate is the process of officially proving the validity of a Will. When a person dies someone else has to deal with their estate whether they died with or without a Will. The Probate Registry acts to confirm what forms are necessary for the person who will administer the Will to fill out, enabling the Probate Registry to confirm that the Will is valid and legally binding.

If a person dies intestate (without a Will) there will be no named executors to carry out their wishes. Somebody else will therefore have to take responsibility, and in order to do so legally they will have to obtain letters of administration. The same would apply to someone named as an executor, but who is unable or unwilling to take on the responsibility. On the other hand, if

Table 1: Bank charges to act as executor

Bank	£250,000 estate	£500,000 estate	£1 million estate
Barclays	£9,500	£14,500	£24,500
HSBC	£10,000	£17,500	£22,500
Lloyds TSB	£10,000	£20,000	£35,000
NatWest	£10,000	£20,000	£25,000
Solicitor	£3,500	£7,500	£15,000

Based on a complicated estate

there is a Will and there are named executors, then they will need to obtain a grant of probate. Either way, the probate office must grant certain documents before you proceed.

Obtaining probate

The executor of the Will can apply for a grant of probate or a solicitor can do it. Fees are generally about £100 per hour and 1% of the estate. If an executor does it without the aid of a solicitor they will need to pay a fee of £130 and any inheritance tax outstanding. This has to be paid before probate is granted and before the Will can be administered.

Grants of administration

These are normally granted to one or more persons who are entitled to a share in the estate of a deceased person who has died without leaving a Will. It can also be granted to a person (individual or company) acting on behalf of such persons, such as a solicitor.

Grants of probate

These are normally granted to the executor of a legally valid Will. The executor will administer the estate subject to the wishes of the deceased.

The requirements of the Probate Registry

In order to claim either document you will need to provide the Probate Registry with the following:
- The death certificate.
- Name, address and occupation of the

proposed administrator.
- A declaration of the total value of the assets.
- Payment of inheritance tax.

Trusts – what are they?

These are often used to set aside funds for children without allowing them access to the capital until they reach a specified age, usually 18 or older depending on the funds. This can be difficult as there is now a market in beneficiaries selling their future interest when they reach the age of 18 if they wish. Ways to avoid this are to use discretionary and protective trusts. A discretionary trust means that the trustees have discretion as to when the capital is handed over. If there is no future certain date, then no one is likely to buy the future interest. A protective trust is designed to protect a beneficiary from themselves. A clause can be inserted to disqualify someone from eventually inheriting if they sell their interest or become bankrupt. Speak to a solicitor.

Most information provided by Online Legal Services. See www.willyouever.co.uk. This information is a guide and should not be taken as definitive legal advice. Speak to a solicitor.

FINANCIAL HELP

"Dying is a very dull, dreary affair. And my advice to you is to have nothing whatever to do with it." W Somerset Maugham (d.1965) was quite right, and never more so when it comes to the financial implications and arrangements that have to be grappled with. Here, briefly, are some of those implications.

Funeral costs

The last time anyone surveyed funeral costs around the country was in the year 2000. Then it was about £1,347. The average cost of a burial was £1,657 and the average cost of a cremation £1,101. However, there were considerable variations, with the average cost in the East Midlands being £1,620 while in London it was £2,391. As all funeral directors will tell you, it's not cheap and costs are not falling. Watch out for hidden extras and ensure you get confirmation in writing from the funeral director as to all the costs. For instance, bear in mind the cost of hearses against the actual need for them.

Most funeral directors require payment before probate (official proof that a Will is valid) is granted and it may be worth considering how to pay for a funeral in advance, if that amount of money is not going to be readily available and there are a number of ways the cost can be covered.

Kate Burchill, of If I Should Die, suggests the following:

1. Check whether the deceased person had contributed to a scheme to pay for a funeral.
2. Check the deceased's papers for a Cremation Society certificate, life-insurance policy papers or details of any pre-paid funeral plan. Also look for letters from previous employers with details about any occupational pension scheme or personal pension.
3. If no one is able, or willing, to arrange and pay for the funeral, the local council, or in some cases the health authority, may do so, but only where the funeral has not already been arranged.

Funeral Payment

This benefit is dealt with by Jobcentre Plus. It helps towards the cost of a funeral and depends on your circumstances, not those of the person who has died. It's a one-off payment. Qualification depends on you answering yes to one of the following:
Are you or your partner getting:
Income Support?
Income-based Jobseeker's Allowance?
Pension Credit?
Housing Benefit?
Council Tax Benefit?
Child Tax Credit which includes an amount higher than the family element?
Working Tax Credit where a disability or severe disability element is included in the award?

Other rules include that you must have taken responsibility for the costs of the funeral and the funeral must usually be in the UK. You can apply any time after the date the person died and up to three months after the date of the funeral. The payment covers: "The necessary cost of specified items or services. Plus up to £700 for other funeral expenses." Contact your Jobcentre Plus office or social security office for more information.

Advice from the Inland Revenue part 1: personal representatives

When a person dies, their personal representative has to sort out their estate. This includes dealing with any assets and paying any debts and unpaid taxes.

If a solicitor is acting on your behalf, or on behalf of the person who has died, the Inland Revenue suggests that you discuss who will be responsible for doing what to sort out the estate.

The personal representative could be a relative of the person who has died or a friend, solicitor or accountant. They are also known as: 1) executors − named in the deceased's Will; or 2) administrators − appointed by the court.

Your responsibilities: If you are the personal representative, you are responsible for managing any income from the estate, sorting out the tax affairs of the person who has died up to the date of death and paying the following: 1) any income tax due on income from the estate; 2) any inheritance tax; 3) any capital gains tax on the sale of property and possessions; 4) any debts,

including unpaid tax. You are also responsible for collecting any money owed to the person who has died, including tax refunds, selling property or any possessions, and distributing the property in the estate to the beneficiaries.

Advice from the Inland Revenue part 2: what to do first?

If you do not have a solicitor what you need to do first depends on whether or not there is a Will, and the value of the estate. For estates under £5,000 without a Will, contact any Inland Revenue office. For estates under £5,000 with a Will or over £5,000 with or without a Will, phone the Inland Revenue's Probate and Inheritance Tax Helpline on 0845 30 20 900. It offers advice and sends out information about inheritance tax, applying for a grant of probate (if there is a Will) and applying for letters of administration (if there is no Will).

Advice from the Inland Revenue part 3: what to do next?

Next you must contact the tax office of the person who has died. Any branch will help you locate their office. All you need to give it is the person's National Insurance number, their name and address, and your name and address.

Taxman

Inheritance tax may be payable on an estate when someone dies or when assets are transferred into a discretionary trust, or to a company. For the majority of estates, more than

96%, there will be no tax to pay because they are below the threshold, but all that will change over time as house prices rise. To find out all you need to know about inheritance tax and a whole lot more, contact the Inland Revenue at Capital Taxes Office, Ferrers House, PO Box 38, Castle Meadow Road, Nottingham NG2 1BB or online at www.inlandrevenue.gov.uk/cto

What is your estate?

A person's estate for the purposes of inheritance tax includes everything owned in their name, their share of anything owned jointly, gifts from which they have kept back some benefit (for example a house still lived in and maintained, although given to someone else) and assets held in trust, from which they get some personal benefit (for example an income).

Seven-year itch

Gifts made to children or relatives more than seven years before a death are exempt from inheritance tax. This raises tricky issues for a family. Simply bringing up the subject may be considered inappropriate, but the bottom line is simple: sort it out early and the taxman won't benefit. Other exemptions:

- Gifts to spouses.
- Gifts not exceeding £3,000 in any one tax year.
- Wedding gifts.
- Gifts to UK charities.
- Gifts for national purposes.
- Small gifts.

- Gifts that are normal expenditure out of income.

Who pays inheritance tax?

The person who administers a deceased person's estate. If there is a Will and the personal representative is named in it they are known as an executor. If there is no Will, or they are appointed by the court, they are known as an administrator. Beware of taking on executor duties.

Advice from the Inland Revenue part 4: who else to contact regarding the deceased's finances?

If the person who has died was self-employed and paid National Insurance contributions by direct debit or quarterly bill you must cancel these arrangements. Phone the National Insurance Contributions Office on 0191 213 5000.

If the person who has died was repaying a student loan, phone the Student Loan Company on 0800 405010.

If the person who has died was claiming tax credits, phone the Tax Credits Helpline on 0845 300 3900.

If the person who has died was claiming child benefit, phone the Child Benefit Office on 0845 302 1444.

If the person who has died was your partner, parent or child, you may be able to claim bereavement benefits. Phone 01304 868 000 for more information or contact the Department for Work and Pensions.

If the person who has died was unemployed,

Example calculation of inheritance tax

Mr Jones died on 10 April 2005 leaving £1,000 to a UK-registered charity and the rest of his estate to his daughter. The threshold for inheritance tax at the time was £275,000 and the rate of IHT is 40%.

Assets value		Allowable deductions		
House	£230,000	Telephone bill	£55	
Car	£9,500	Electricity bill	£45	
Bank account	£19,250	Gas bill	£35	
Shares	£30,075	Funeral expenses	£950	
Premium Bonds	£500			
		Total deductions	£1,085	
Total value	= £289,325	Less charity exemption	£1,000	
		Net value of estate	£287,240	

Inheritance Tax is payable because the net value of the estate is above the threshold of £275,000. Tax is charged at 40%.

Net value of assets	£287,240
Less threshold	£275,000
Total liable to tax	£12,240

Inheritance Tax (£12,240x40%)
=£4,896

---

contact the Department for Work and Pensions or their local office.

If the person who has died was getting a state pension, phone the Pensions Service on 08456 060265 or contact the Department for Work and Pensions.

Bereavement Allowance

A new system of bereavement benefits for men and women was introduced in April 2001. The new system will not affect women who were already getting benefits under the previous scheme, as long as they qualify under the rules. A Bereavement Allowance is based on your late husband or wife's NI contributions and paid for 52 weeks from the date of bereavement. To qualify, you must be: 1) a widow or widower who was aged 45 or over when your husband or wife died; 2) not bringing up children; 3) under state-pension age. The standard rate is £82.05. For more information, visit: www.jobcentreplus.gov.uk

Bereavement Payment (formerly Widow's Payment)

A Bereavement Payment is based on your late husband's or wife's NI contributions and is a one-off payment. To get it, you must say yes to two of the following:

Are you under the age of 60 for women, or 65 for men (state pension age)?

Are you the widow of a man or widower of a woman who was not entitled to a category A Retirement Pension when they died?

Are you the widow or widower of a spouse who

has paid NI contributions?

The payment is a lump sum of £2,000. Contact your Jobcentre Plus office or social security office for more information.

Occupational and personal pensions

If your husband or wife paid into a pension scheme through his job, or he or she paid into a personal pension scheme, you may be entitled to receive a widow's or widower's pension from the scheme. Generally, you will receive a proportion of the amount your husband or wife was entitled to. However, each pension scheme is different. The pension company should give you full details about what you will receive, once you tell them about your husband or wife's death. Any pension you receive through your husband's or wife's occupational or personal pension scheme will not affect your entitlement to a State Retirement Pension, Bereavement Payment, or Bereavement Allowance.

Whole of life insurance

It is also worth considering whole of life insurance as a means of paying inheritance tax bills. This form of cover guarantees the payment of a fixed lump sum on the death of the policy holder. This can make a whole of life policy particularly suitable for inheritance tax planning because it takes away the uncertainty.

Unlike term assurance, whole of life cover does not guarantee fixed-premium levels throughout the term. Premiums are normally reviewed after ten years and afterwards at even more frequent levels by the insurance company,

determined by how many policyholders have died and investment performance.

Whole of life policies written in trust can also be used to reduce delays on money left between spouses, bypassing probate and avoiding inheritance tax liabilities that may occur on the second death within a married couple.

Many whole of life insurance policies offer a high degree of flexibility, with the opportunity to increase cover levels and to continue cover but cease paying premiums at a certain age, such as retirement.

Money saving

- You do not have to have a funeral ceremony.
- You do not have to have a religious minister.
- You do not have to use a funeral director.
- A ceremony does not have to take place in a crematorium or place of worship.

Banks can help

It is a good idea to speak with your bank manager or a representative from your local branch in the weeks following a bereavement. Some offer good advice about all aspects of bereavement (Barclays publishes a useful leaflet), in terms of financial and practical help. It also makes sense to talk to someone from the bank about reorganising finances. It's not a great prospect talking to the bank about the death of a loved one but it shouldn't be put off only to put you in financial difficulty on top of everything else. Banks should be able to arrange mortgage holidays and other methods for dealing with the consequences of a death.

CONTACTS, ORGANISATION, ASSOCIATIONS, CHARITIES, SUPPORT GROUPS... AND EVERYTHING

Age Concern
207 Pentonville Road, London N1
T 020 7278 1114
W www.helptheaged.org.uk
Fact sheets and information on all aspects of death and bereavement, also offers a Will-writing service.

Benefits Agency
Find local office in local phone directory under social security or benefits agency. Or call the Public Enquiry Office on 020 7712 2171.
W www.dss.gov.uk
Relevant leaflets and advice on claiming benefits.

British Association for Counselling and Psychotherapy
BACP House, 35-37 Albert St, Rugby, Warwickshire CV21 2SG
T 01788 578328/9
W www.counselling.co.uk
Provides details of counselling organisations and services in your area.

British Humanist Association
1 Gower St, London WC1E 6HD
T 020 7079 3580
W www.humanism.org.uk
Information on non-religious funerals.

British Institute of Embalmers
21c, Station Road, Knowle, Solihull. West Midlands B93 OHL.
T 01564 778991
W www.bioe.co.uk

British Organ Donor Society
Balsham, Cambridge CB1 6DL
T 01223 893636
W www.bodyuk.org
Information and general inquiries as well as support for donor and recipient families.

The Child Bereavement Trust
Aston House, West Wycombe, High Wycombe, Bucks HP14 3AG
T 0845 357 1000 (information & support)
W www.childbereavement.org.uk

Child Death Support Helpline
c/o Great Ormond Street Hospital, Great Ormond Street, London WC1N 3JH
T 0800 282 986 (helpline)
W www.childdeathhelpline.org.uk

Cinnamon Trust
10 Market Square, Hayle, Cornwall TR27 4HE
T 01736 7579000
W www.cinnamon.org.uk
Cares for pets belonging to the elderly and terminally ill.

Citizens Advice
Myddelton House, 115-123 Pentonville Road, London, N1 9LZ (head office)
W www.citizensadvice.org.uk
Check your local directory for a CAB nearby. Offer all sorts of confidential help and advice about death, bereavement and financial matters.

Compassionate Friends
53 North Street, Bristol BS3 1EN
T 0845 123 2304 (helpline)
W www.tcf.org.uk
Support for bereaved parents.

Cremation Society of Great Britain
Brecon House, 16a Albion Place, Maidstone, Kent ME14 5DZ.

T 01622 688292/3
W www.cremation.org.uk
The aim of the society: "To promote and establish the practice of cremation for the disposal of the bodies of dead persons and to join with local authorities or other bodies or persons for this purpose."

Cruse Bereavement Care
Cruse House, 126 Sheen Road, Richmond, Surrey TW9 1UR.
T 020 8939 8939
0870 1671677 (to speak to a counsellor afternoons or evenings)
W www.crusebereavementcare.org.uk
Provides help to the bereaved. It runs helplines and support groups. Also publishes many publications.

Depression Alliance
212 Spitfire Studios, 63-71 Collier Street, London N1 9BE (head office)
T 0845 123 23 20.
W www.depressionalliance.org
Publishes guides, runs network of self-help groups and provides penfriends for depressed people.

Direct Marketing Association
DMA House, 70 Margaret Street, London, W1W 8SS
T 020 7291 3300
W www.dma.org.uk
Deceased still getting post from mail order companies? This is their trade body.

Disaster Action
PO Box 849, Woking GU21 8WB
T 01483 799066
W www.disasteraction.org.uk
Self-help group for those bereaved by a major disaster such as a plane crash or tsunami.

Drowning Support Network
W http://health.groups.yahoo.com/group/DrowningSupportNetwork

Online message board offering support for those bereaved in incidents involving drowning or other aquatic accidents.

Equine Cremation Services
Midleton Road, Guildford, Surrey GU2 8XW
T 01483 505524
W www.equine-cremations.co.uk

www.findagrave.com
Famous, infamous, international, local. A bit odd. Set up by American Jim Tipton. Talking about his "favourite graves" he comments: "Richard Feynman (one of my all time favourites), Al Jolson (for its unsubtle grandeur), Lucille Ball (for its modesty)."

The Guild of Taxidermists
c/o Glasgow Museums, Resource Centre 200, Woodhead Road, South Nitshill, Glasgow G53 7NN
T 0141 267 9445
W www.taxidermy.org.uk

Help the Aged
16-18 St James's Walk, London EC1R 0BE
T 0207 253 0253
W www.helptheaged.org.uk
Information and advice for older people and their families, including on financial implications of a bereavement.

Help the Hospices
Hospice House, 34-44 Britannia Street, London WC1X 9JG
T 020 7520 8200
W www.helpthehospices.org.uk
It should be to the eternal shame of each and every British Government that the hospice movement in the UK is entirely dependent on charity. So long as the situation remains this way, hospices need financial support.

If I Should Die.co.uk
W www.ifishoulddie.co.uk
Set up by Kate Burchill, this is an excellent website covering all aspects of bereavement from the practical to the emotional.

Jewish Bereavement Counselling Service
8/10 Forty Avenue, Wembley HA9 8JW.
T   0208 385 1874
W   www.jvisit.org.uk/jbcs
Counselling services for the Jewish faith.

Lesbian and Gay Bereavement Project
Vaughan Williams Centre, Colindale Hospital,
London NW9 5GH
T   020 7403 5969 (helpline)

Light Aircraft Crash Bereavement Support
T   01200 429346
W   www.lacbs.i12.com
Founded by Madeline Adey, herself bereaved in this manner.

Marine Consents & Environment Unit
3-8 Whitehall Place, (2nd Floor – Area D), London, SW1A 2HH
W   www.mceu.gov.uk
Deals with bureaucracy surrounding burial at sea.

Memorials by Artists
Snape Priory, Snape, Suffolk IP17 1SA.
T   01728 688934
W   www.memorialsbyartists.co.uk
Founded by Harriet Frazer, it provides a nationwide service that helps people to commission individual memorials. It's an excellent idea and is well worth checking out.

Miscarriage Association
c/o Clayton Hospital, Northgate, Wakefield,
West Yorkshire WF1 3JS
T   01924 200 799 (helpline)
W   www.miscarriageassociation.org.uk
Runs support groups and helplines, and provides information.

National Association of Funeral Directors
618 Warwick Road, Solihull, West Midlands B91 1AA
T   0845 230 1343.
W   www.nafd.org.uk

National Association of Widows
48 Queens Road, Coventry CV1 3EH
T   0845 838 2261
W   www.nawidows.org.uk
Offers widow-to-widow support, comfort and advice.

National Federation of Cemetery Friends
W   www.cemeteryfriends.fsnet.co.uk
Groups of volunteers dedicated to preserving their local cemeteries. Most cemeteries desperately need volunteer help so get involved, preserve a piece of history and enjoy the outside.

National Society of Allied & Independent Funeral Directors
3 Bullfields, Sawbridgeworth, Herts CM21 9DB
T   0845 230 6777
W   www.saif.org.uk

The Natural Death Centre
6 Blackstock Mews, Blackstock Road, London N4 2BT.
T   0871 288 2098
W   www.naturaldeath.org.uk
Promotes environmental side of funeral business and publishes various publications, including the very excellent *New Natural Death Handbook*.

www.pushindaisies.com
An online mortuary novelty shop, it sells all manner of death-related goods.

RoadPeace
PO Box 2579, London NW10 3PW
T   0845 450 0355 (helpline)
W   www.roadpeace.org
RoadPeace is a UK charity supporting road traffic victims and their families. It provides practical and emotional support and information.

Royal Society for the Prevention of Accidents
RoSPA House, Edgbaston Park, 353 Bristol Road,

Edgbaston, Birmingham B5 7ST
T   0121 248 2000
W   www.rospa.org.uk

Royal College of Pathologists
2 Carlton House Terrace, London SW1Y 5AF.
T   020 7451 6700
W   www.rcpath.org

Samaritans
The Upper Mill, Kingston Road, Ewell, Surrey, KT17 2AF.
(head office)
T   08457 909090
W   www.samaritans.org.uk
Provides 24-hour telephone helpline to people in difficulty.

Shipwrecked Mariners' Society
1 North Pallant, Chichester, West Sussex PO19 1TL.
T   01243 789329 (admin)
W   www.shipwreckedmariners.org.uk
It is a registered charity whose object is to "relieve distress amongst the seafaring community by making grants to merchant seafarers and fishermen, their widows and dependants in cases of need".

Stillbirth and Neonatal Death Society
28 Portland Place, London W1B 1LY
T   020 7436 5881 (helpline)
W   www.uk-sands.org
Provides national network of help and support for bereaved parents and families who have suffered the death of a baby either before, during, or shortly after birth.

Support after murder and manslaughter
Cranmer House, 39 Brixton Road, London SW9 6DZ
T   0207 735 3838
W   www.samm.org.uk
Support and a confidential telephone helpline offering support and information to anyone affected by murder or manslaughter.

Survivors of Bereavement by Suicide
Centre 88, Saner Street, Hull, HU3 2TR.
T   0870 241 3337.
W   www.uk-sobs.org.uk
It offers emotional and practical support, including bereavement packs, group meetings, conferences, residential events and information relating to practical issues and problems. A voluntary organisation, it is staffed by many who have themselves been bereaved by suicide.

Dignity in Dying
13 Prince of Wales Terrace, London W8 5PG.
T   020 7937 7770
W   www.dignityindying.org.uk
It promotes greater patient choice at the end of life.

The WAY Foundation
PO Box 6767, Brackley NN13 6YW
T   0870 0113 450
W   www.wayfoundation.org.uk
A self-help support network for men and women widowed up to the age of 50.

Winston's Wish
Clara Burgess Centre, Bayshill Road, Cheltenham GL50 3AW
T   01242 515157
W   www.winstonswish.org.uk
Last but certainly not least. It supports bereaved children. Highly recommended.

PICTURE STORIES

Dead serious

1) Callum Sutherland. Interviewed at a film set for Linda LaPlante TV series in which he acted as forensic adviser. The photo itself was shot in south-east London at an actual murder scene.

3) Abu Sayeed. Recommended to me by my former driving instructor Fizz, Abu Sayeed is a highly respected and educated imam. The picture was taken at Great Ormond Street Hospital.

4) Kevin Bocquet. One of the hardest people to arrange to photograph, Bocquet is a man in demand. The picture was taken by a canal in Manchester.

5) Paul Sinclair. The image is shot at Donnington Park Grand Prix Circuit. Sinclair had previously driven the body of a former employee around the circuit as a final wish and the management kindly allowed us on the track on a race day.

7) Oliver Goldmeyer. A contact of Eric Langham's, Goldmeyer kindly allowed me into his home and spent several hours explaining Judaism and death to me (a bold undertaking).

9) Howard Jonas. Shot in the pet cemetery, Cambridge. Jonas's office is at a site backing on to Duxford airfield, giving the impression, every ten minutes, that it was being dive-bombed by single-engine aircraft.

Dead calm

1) Ian Hill. The fliers pinned up on the wall behind him are of the various television and film productions on which Hill has advised. Thanks to Hannah.

2) Chandu Tailor. When showing me around his premises, Tailor pointed towards the chapel that he was later photographed in. "There's a coffin in there," he said. What he didn't explain was that the coffin was open and there was a dead woman in it.

5) Michael Burgess. Although agreeing to be interviewed, Burgess refused to be photographed because of his dislike of publicity.

7) Richard Harries. The picture was shot in the bishops' office

in the House of Lords. When interviewing Harries at his offices in Oxford, some of his staff assumed I was another Jamie Oliver and brought cookery books in for me to sign.

8) John Sheils. Sheils, a practical joker, and his wife live directly above the mortuary.

9) Andrew McKie. The picture was taken at Canary Wharf, London, where The Daily Telegraph's offices are situated. In the obituaries department there is a wall of cabinets full of information on prominent people yet to die.

Dead & buried

1) Roslyn Cassidy. The first picture taken, ably assisted by Jackie, was shot in the pouring rain in the woodland buried section of the City of London cemetery.

5) Gary and Beryl Doswell. The picture was taken in East Sussex. At one stage, photographer Cristian and his assistant had to pack up their equipment and run when one of the relatives headed over to see how the grave-digging was progressing.

6) Penny and Caroline Black. The picture is of the two sisters-in-law on swings in a park in Chiswick, London.

7) John Harris. The picture is shot in Barking, east London and features two Belgium Black, or Friesian, horses, owned by T Crib & Son.

Dead ahead

2) Joyce and Ivan Fox. The picture was taken in a street in Nottingham. The name "Crazy Coffins" was something dreamt up by the Sun newspaper. The company is actually called Vic Fearn and Co.

4) Dorothy and Jeremy Moore Brookes. The picture was shot in their Hertfordshire home. And what a lovely couple they are!

9) Dave Bingham. Ahead of the interview with Bingham, he explained on the phone that it sounded like an interesting idea and that, actually, he had died earlier in the year. Which was a little disconcerting, but unique.

INDEX

Page numbers in bold refer to photographs/illustrations